With /

Myer Elliot

A Glimpse into an Ordinary, Yet Extraordinary Life

Genuine people are not larger than life. It's just that they fill up a life when it's well-lived. The man this book calls Anders Erickssen is such a person. His story is filled with incidents, large and small, that welcome us. They bring us closer to him, and we come to know and to admire the person inside the story.

From his humble, small-town beginnings and boyhood during the Depression, Anders frankly shares his adventures…and misadventures. His experiences do not set us apart from him, they draw us to him in their poignancy, humor, and humanness.

The flavor of the locations and the eras Anders travels through are brought to life, from semi-rugged upstate California, to Berkeley, to a stint at Guantanamo Bay, where his integrity gets him into trouble instead of keeping him out of it.

We finally settle in Southern California, where the story gives a different perspective on the reality of doctors and wealth, and it reveals much of the evolution of modern heart medicine. It most definitely did not happen the way we might think.

Incident after real incident, event after recognizable event, we walk with Anders through his life. We see the world we all share through different, sometimes wide and innocent eyes. And we come to respect the amazing accomplishments made in the field of heart medicine by this eminently human man.

The story of Anders Erickssen, truly the story of the author, is encouraging, inspiring, and reassuring that a life can be lived with goodness and integrity, respecting all people and contributing to their betterment.

This is a book to be read when you feel like having a heartfelt conversation with a good friend.

Skiing in Aspen at 84 years of age.

D r. Myrvin Ellestad has built a life worthy of respect and admiration, both in his professional career and in his personal endeavors. In addition to being in the forefront of heart-related medical developments, he has enjoyed membership in many prestigious medical organizations, won awards too numerous to list here, and served in top positions in hospitals and university faculties. An octogenarian as of this writing, he remains very active in his personal and professional life. Dr. Ellestad lives in Southern California with his wife and large family of grown children and grandchildren. The story of Anders Erickssen is patterned after his own.

A ROMANCE WITH THE HEART

A ROMANCE
WITH
THE HEART

*An Intimate Look at the Life and Work
of a Pioneer in Heart Medicine*

MYRVIN ELLESTAD, M.D.

CEDAR VISTA

BEVERLY HILLS, CALIFORNIA

A Romance with the Heart: An Intimate Look at the Life and Work of a
Pioneer in Heart Medicine

 Published in the United States by Cedar Vista Trade
Paperback Originals, an imprint of Little Moose Press,
a division of Smarketing LLC, California.

For information, address Cedar Vista, 269 South Beverly Drive
Suite #1065, Beverly Hills, CA 90212, 866-234-0626.
www.cedarvistabooks.com.

This is a memoir; however, some names and places have been altered to
protect the privacy of the individual.

Library of Congress Cataloging-in-Publication Data

Ellestad, Myrvin H., 1921-

    A romance with the heart / Myrvin Ellestad. -- 1st ed.
    p. cm.
    ISBN 0-9786049-8-9 (trade pbk. : alk. paper)
    1. Ellestad, Myrvin H., 1921- 2. Cardiologists--United States--
Biography. I. Title.
RC666.72.E45A3 2006
616.1'20092--dc22
[B]   2006020954

Book Designer: Patricia Bacall
Editor: Brookes Nohlgren

Printed and bound in the United States of America on acid-free paper.

FOREWORD

A *Romance with the Heart* is a true story about a small-town boy who believed that his doctor, Max Dunovitz, not only rescued him from illness but also was a friend he could strive to emulate.

The pseudonym *Anders Erickssen* was selected, as were many of the other names used in the story, to add local color and to reduce the personal impact of some of the episodes included. Many of those who played a prominent role in my life will undoubtedly appreciate that they remain anonymous.

My childhood, in a small mountain town during the Depression, characterizes a time in America when children had more freedom than they do now but, at the same time, were expected to be more responsible. Their recreation was unstructured and was often a product of their own imagination, and thus they learned to be more creative. The close-knit community of this small mountain town provided a certain security for children that in some ways allowed them more leeway, yet created the understanding that they would be held responsible for their actions.

In my case, as I matured and became immersed in medicine, it stimulated me to envision what was on the horizon and therefore to contribute to the progress being made.

The second half of the twentieth century was a time when cardiology evolved into one of the most important branches of medicine and, although I had no formal training in this specialty, I was able to make a major contribution to the knowledge base, and meet and become friends with many of the men who were breaking new ground. Today the specialty of cardiology requires at least three years of formal training after a program in internal medicine is completed.

I hope you will enjoy a peek into my boyhood, my personal life, and some of the unusual experiences in my professional life as well. I believe this story illustrates that energy and involvement can provide the opportunity, even for a small-town boy, to live a life that is fulfilling and that makes a difference.

I am indebted to my loyal secretary, Carole Sweet, who labored over the many iterations of this manuscript. And to my wonderful wife, Lera, who has always been supportive of every endeavor I have undertaken.

ONE

A NASTY, COLD WINTER

The winter of 1928 was one of the coldest of the decade in the California Sierra Nevada Mountains. The foothill town of Auburn, then populated with about 2,000 people, was under almost two feet of snow, and higher up, near Donner Summit, the snow pack had reached thirty feet. Even the Southern Pacific Railroad, in many places covered by miles of snowsheds, had several weeks when trains could not get through.

Anders Erickssen, a skinny towhead now seven years old, and the other kids in the neighborhood had made snowmen, had snowball fights, and slid down the hills in town on their home-made skis. The small Norwegian colony that had settled there to work in the lumber mills had already made skiing about as popular as basketball was in Indiana, and whenever there was snow there was skiing.

One day after spending several hours in the snow, Anders developed a high fever and a very sore throat. Soon he could hardly swallow and had shaking chills, which racked his rather skinny body.

A mustard plaster was applied and saltwater gargles were instituted, but when no relief came after two days and considerable consultation with Melvin, Anders' father, Anders' mother called Dr. Russell, Auburn's only doctor, who had to put chains on his car to come to the house but finally arrived for an examination. By this time Anders had intermittent vomiting and his urine had turned brown. Dr. Russell, after a careful examination, announced that Anders had strep throat and Bright's disease and, along with this, rheumatic heart disease.

Dr. Russell explained that the brown urine and swelling around Anders' face indicated that the streptococcus had infected the kidneys, and a heart murmur indicated that the strep had also attacked the heart valves. He described the situation as very serious because streptococcus, for which there was no treatment, together with kidney disease (glomerulonephritis) and valvular heart disease was a very bad combination. Streptococcus caused rheumatic fever, a condition affecting the heart valves, as well as kidney disease, a very common problem in the twenties and thirties. Unfortunately, this was twenty-five years before the discovery of penicillin. It was a gloomy time in the Erickssen household.

Aspirin, tepid baths, bed rest, and a liquid diet were prescribed. Somewhat to Dr. Russell's surprise, Anders began to improve. The puffiness in his face, the high fever and chills, and the brown urine all gradually went away, everything but the heart murmur. On Dr. Russell's next visit he announced that Anders would probably survive, but would be left with a damaged heart and would have to be kept in bed. For how long? Maybe several months! So a bed was moved from the bedroom to the kitchen, where the family could keep an eye on him. And so, the family made plans for a long illness.

Anders' mother, an elementary school teacher, and his father, a high school teacher, organized their lives around their son, who, though frail in appearance, seemed to be improving rapidly. The winter wore on, the snow melted and spring came. Anders looked better to his parents, who were enthusiastic about his progress, but they both were worried about his schooling. Anders did not like staying in bed even though Dr. Russell had advised him, "Your heart is still bad, and the only thing that will help is bed rest." Spring passed, summer came, and Anders' mother was busy running to the library. Anders was reading everything his mother could carry home. She arranged for her teacher friends to come by and give him lessons. She kept saying, "When he gets well he won't be behind in his schoolwork." Thus, Anders became an avid reader.

Summer had arrived. Anders' father was planning to build a rental house during the school vacation on a vacant lot down the hill from their fifty-year-old residence. Each year he planned some project for the three-month vacation when school was out but would always take time for a family camping trip somewhere in the Sierras or possibly Yosemite or even as far away as Yellowstone Park.

One day Melvin came home with some important news. A new doctor had come to town. A young fellow who had just graduated from the University of California Medical School in San Francisco. Now Auburn had two doctors. Maybe Max Dunovitz, the new doctor, would know how to cure Anders' heart trouble. Melvin visited the newly opened office and arranged for Dr. Dunovitz to come by and examine Anders.

The day of Max Dunovitz's house call to the Erickssens' was a day for celebration. After a careful examination he said, "If Anders ever had heart disease, I believe it is healed. All he has now is a functional murmur. Get him out of bed. I believe he can live a normal life."

In the years to come Max Dunovitz, the second doctor in Auburn, became a very important person in the Erickssen household and a role model for Anders. As the years passed, Anders would spend time sitting in Dr. Dunovitz's office watching him examine and treat patients. As Anders grew and finished grammar and high school and planned for college he knew he had to become a doctor. For Anders, there seemed to be no other choice. Many times while attending Berkeley, Anders would come home to Auburn especially to receive advice and counsel from Max.

– TWO –

THE FISHERMAN

Three years had passed since the rheumatic attack of fever and kidney disease, and Anders seemed to be completely recovered. Occasionally Dr. Dunovitz would examine him and remark that his functional murmur seemed to be improving, and Anders was not aware of any physical limitations. Hiking and fishing had become important summer activities for the Erickssen family and Anders had taken up skiing in the winter.

A long weekend in the mountains was always an exciting event. This particular weekend in midsummer 1932 was to be a camp out at Big Bend, a public campground on the upper reaches of the Yuba River. This beautiful mountain river, less than thirty miles from its source near Donner Summit, the major route from California to Nevada, which winds through a verdant valley about ten miles long, consists of numerous pools separated by short rapids. The bank is heavily wooded with madrone, spruce, and sugar pine. Numerous large rocks along the bank create eddies and overhangs, where rainbow and German brown trout abound.

Anders' family—consisting of father Melvin, Melvin's brother, John, Anders' mother, Myrtle, and baby sister, Elaine—were frequent campers and avid fishermen. Melvin and John always competed for the largest fish and the first to limit. As a ten-year-old, Anders had limited skills but his enthusiasm was unbounded.

Uncle John, by far the best fisherman in the family, was always full of jokes explaining his success, the most memorable being that the fish would bite if you hold your mouth a certain way. This, followed by a series of facial contortions, would send everyone into hysterics.

The first day fishing was typical of midsummer in the Sierras—cold in the morning, warm and sunny all day, and cool enough for a campfire and a jacket in the evening. The first evening was always an event—listening to the fish stories and eating the pan-fried trout along with the usual fried potatoes, brown beans, and mother's wonderful apple pie. Anders longed to be the center of attention in the fish stories but was always overshadowed by Uncle John, who almost always had the biggest fish and the funniest tales. For Anders, the first day of fishing on this particular trip was a total disappointment and a terrible event. Over and over he watched as John and his father brought in one trout after another. None were very large, but they were excellent eight- to ten-inch pan-sized fish. Anders went all day without a single bite. Not catching any fish was bad enough, but listening to Uncle John's jokes about why Anders couldn't catch a fish was absolutely defeating. Since Anders' father and John had caught their limit by mid afternoon they all went back to camp, where Anders watched the fish being cleaned, smarting under the stigma of being a failure. As the evening shadows began to lengthen, he decided to go down to the river by himself in a desperate effort to qualify for approval as a fisherman. Less than half a mile from camp he came upon an exciting spectacle. Swimming in an eddy, close to the bank, was the biggest rainbow trout he had ever seen. The fish was obviously dying—swimming on its side in a feeble attempt to survive. After Anders dangled a hook in front of the fish for a minute or two, it was obvious that it was far beyond taking the fly. Finally Anders was able to lodge the tip of his pole under its gill and steer it to shore, where he pounced on it and laid it out on the grass. Without so much as a flop it died almost instantly.

As he stood there, Anders imagined what a hero he would be bringing in this monster fish, much bigger than any the others had caught that day. Yet, he was worried that the fish might not be safe to eat if it had been sick, and he knew he would be quizzed in detail as to how much of a fight the fish had put up, what kind of a fly he had used, and whether others like it were nearby, and so forth. No matter, here was his chance to have a fish bigger than anyone else had, even Uncle John. The fish was about twenty-four inches long and weighed over five pounds. Anders grabbed the fish, jabbed the fly into its lip, and started running back to camp. When he got within earshot, he started hollering that he was the champion fisherman of the day.

The amazement and surprise, congratulations and celebrations by his mother that he was a better fisherman than anyone else, were gratifying. He concocted a story of how the fish had hit his fly twice before being hooked, how he thought his pole would break as he battled it to the shore, which assured his place as the center of attention. Anders' mother proceeded to clean the fish and into the pan it went with the others, which looked like minnows by comparison.

As darkness settled over the camp Anders' mother served the fish to Anders with great fanfare. At about this time he began to wonder why the fish had died and whether he might too if he ate it. All of a sudden Anders burst into tears and confessed to his big lie. There was dead silence about the campfire. Anders got up, ran to his tent, and laid on the cot, sobbing. No one came to console or punish him. Later that night when his family finally came to the tent to go to sleep his father sat on the edge of the cot and said, "Son, we are all ashamed of what you have done. I hope you will remember this day if you are ever tempted to do something dishonest again." In the Erickssen household, honesty was essential. Dishonesty was an unacceptable sin.

No one in the family ever mentioned the incident again. Did Anders remember the day? It stuck with him for a long time afterward, the sense of guilt and shame lingering for years. Especially bothersome were family fishing trips, so much so that as an older teenager Anders lost the desire to go trout fishing. The other boys in Auburn, a town where fishing was a tradition, couldn't understand his lack of enthusiasm, but much to his relief they never heard the real story.

Only after many years was Anders able to discuss this episode with friends, so vividly was the feeling of embarrassment emblazoned in his memory.

- THREE -

THE CREVICE CLUB

For Auburn youth, early summer was a time for adventure in the Sierras. Anders had put the misadventure of the previous year behind him. Only half a mile from the edge of Auburn, 1,000 feet down the canyon, winds the north fork of the American River. Heavy woods of pine, oak, and madrone as well as various undergrowth make this steep canyon picture postcard beautiful. The wilderness was an exciting playground for the young boys growing up in this quiet little mother lode town east of Sacramento and west of Lake Tahoe.

One hundred feet below the edge of the canyon was a rocky cliff almost 100 feet high that jutted out through the foliage, providing a perch where the river, winding hundreds of feet below, could be viewed. Years before, perhaps thousands, an earthquake or possibly a glacier produced a nearly vertical crack near its middle, separating the north and south sides of the rock by approximately three to four feet. This crack zigzagged up the face of the rock, which protruded about forty feet above the foliage, growing on the wall of the canyon. The eight- to twelve-year-old boys of Auburn called this "the crevice."

The boys discovered that they could climb from the base of the cliff up the crevice by putting their feet on one side of the crack and their back against the other. As one worked his way up or down, spectacular views of a winding river 600-800 feet below were possible, if the boys weren't too scared to look. For years some of the young boys in Auburn had formed a social group called the "Crevice Club." It was a great honor to be a member of this club, but the initiation required that the new boy climb from the bottom to the top in the accompaniment of one or more of the members. This was a secret club and it was required that members never tell their parents about their activities or siblings who might tattle to the parents, or especially girls.

The first trip up the crevice was a very scary experience, but with repetition some of the boys became quite bold, especially when describing it to a prospective new member. One Sunday afternoon Anders was selected along with another member to accompany a new boy in town, about a year younger than Anders, on his first climb up the crevice, thus initiating him into the club. It was agreed that they would meet on the edge of town shortly after church and take the trail to the base of the cliff for this most important endeavor.

Anders, Wally, and Robbie—the new initiate—climbed down the trail where the two club members explained to him the technique of working their way up the rock fissure. They gave him numerous warnings about how dangerous it was, although to their knowledge no one in the club had ever fallen. Robbie, at the base of the cliff, glanced with obvious anxiety down at the river several hundred feet below and decided he would forego the honor of being a member. Wally and Anders of course told him that he would forever be labeled a "chicken," and asked how he would like to have this embarrassing fact known. Certainly it would damage his social standing!

After a few minutes of reassurance, the new initiate was induced to start up the climb. Wally, the oldest, was to lead,

Robbie would go next, and Anders was to bring up the rear. The first thirty feet of the eighty-foot climb were relatively easy, with plenty of rock shelves for their feet and hands. Also, during this part of the climb, you could not yet see the river below. At about halfway, it became necessary to inch up the bulge in a ten-foot segment with feet against one wall and back against the other.

This section of the crevice led to an overhang where one could look down and see the American River about 500 feet below. Wally and Anders were doing their best to impress Robbie on how dangerous this section was when all of a sudden the rock against Anders' back got warm and wet. Robbie, in his fear, had wet his pants, and Anders' shirt and back were soon soggy. Robbie then started to cry and said he couldn't go on. It seemed to Wally and Anders that going up would be easier than going down, but Robbie wouldn't budge. He was terrified.

Wally and Anders shuffled around enough to find some solid footing and proceeded to try to persuade Robbie to go forward. During this period, which may have lasted approximately five minutes yet seemed like an eternity, it started to rain. Within a few minutes the rock walls of the crevice were wet and getting muddy. At this point Wally and Anders were almost as afraid as Robbie was, but they somehow managed to keep their fear hidden. After fifteen or twenty minutes of rain it was obvious it was only going to get worse, and they finally managed to push and prod Robbie up the other thirty feet to the top of the crevice. By this time they were all covered with mud, which Anders preferred to urine.

All three boys were shaking as they finally climbed up and out of the rocky shelf. It was not clear whether it was caused by fear or the cold rain. On the trip up the trail to town they tried to think of a story they would tell their parents to explain why they had been out in the rain and were now covered in mud. Robbie, all of a sudden, was very pleased with himself as he was now a full-fledged member of the Crevice Club. Wally and Anders told him how great he was and how all of their friends would know how brave he had been, and they assured him they would never "rat" on him about the wet pants episode.

As the rain stopped and the sun came out, the experience in the crevice took on a special significance and resulted in a bond of friendship among the three boys that would last for years.

– FOUR –

THE AMERICAN RIVER RIDE

Two years had passed since the fishing episode on the Yuba River. Life in Auburn was idyllic. Everyone knew everyone else. The Depression and the stock market crash of the thirties had almost no impact here. No one was rich and it seemed almost no one was very poor. The school year was over and plans for the summer were underway.

When summer weather comes to the mountains the melting snows in the high Sierras turn the American River into a roaring torrent. This beautiful canyon, almost 1,000 feet deep with a summertime meandering current lined by rocky cliffs and lush beech and pine trees, overnight becomes a crashing maelstrom with the water level rising nearly 100 feet. It carries logs and brush, and the logs act like battering rams, threatening the supports of the bridges connecting the mountain towns along its course.

Within a few weeks, however, the river returns to its former state, depositing the big sugar pine logs along its gravel bars. This was a time when the twelve-year-old Anders and his friends headed for the river to pry the logs back into the water and at times ride them for several miles downstream.

On a warm Sunday afternoon in late June, Anders, Robert, and Wally headed for the river with great expectations and excitement.

The water had receded almost to the summer level and the late spring rains had deposited more logs this year than usual. After covering the three-mile hike from town on the canyon rim the boys were hot and sweaty, and the cold water quenched their thirst as they walked along the bank looking for a suitable vehicle for the much anticipated ride.

After prying a few small logs into the river, the boys came upon a big sugar pine, obviously washed out of some upstream sawmill. It was about four feet in diameter and fifteen feet long and just barely stranded on a gravel bar. Considerable discussion followed. "What if we can't get off before it goes over the dam?" The dam was about five miles downstream. "What if it rolls over in midstream?" Wally, the most aggressive, reassured everyone, saying, "Don't worry, come on, are you guys chicken?" The thought of being a "chicken" settled the issue.

After a monstrous struggle the log was pried into the stream and all three boys climbed on. Within a few minutes they were in swift rapids and all were worried that they had made the wrong choice. Soon they were in a major set of rapids and as the log plunged downstream the boys were soon soaked in the cold water. Within about 100 yards they were all wondering how they could end the trip, when the log was caught in an eddy and started rotating end for end. It appeared it might run aground and allow them to disembark.

As it bounced off a large boulder and rotated toward a gravel bar, it rolled over. Wally and Robert flew off into the shallows, but Anders hung on and was suddenly under the log in about two feet of water. His left arm and shoulder were pinned under the log in the gravel bed and he was just able to get his head above water. As the pain of the weight shot through his body he shouted for help to Robbie and Wally, who were scrambling up the bank. Both boys waded in and struggled with the log, but were unable to lift it off Anders' shoulder and arm. Anders shouted that if they rolled it toward the water he would be forced under. Fear and the cold water augmented his pain and anxiety.

Wally and Robert ran up the bank and secured a large tree limb, which they were able to insert under the log, lifting it enough to set Anders free. As he came out of the water, now red from blood from the crush injury to his arm, the bark of the sugar pine was embedded in the skin of his forearm. Although the pain was somewhat relieved, Anders looked like he might faint. His already pale countenance was chalk white.

As he sat in the shallow water with blood oozing out of his arm, he pictured himself bleeding to death. Robert and Wally bandaged his arm with a cutoff sleeve of his jacket and dragged him out of the water onto the gravel bar. After a few minutes they all decided that they had to get out of the canyon and go for help.

After a short rest Anders looked somewhat better, so they headed back up the river where they knew the logging road they had followed down would lead back up the 1,000-foot canyon wall. Quickly the cold and shivering from the river water combined with the shock of the accident turned to sweat, and some flies attracted by the bloody bandages began swarming around the three boys. As they labored up the three-mile road, fear about the seriousness of Anders' injury somehow fortified their climb. About one hour later the logging road intersected with a country road, where a passing car picked the boys up and delivered them to Anders' home.

Anders' parents were sitting on the front lawn drinking lemonade and visiting with Max Dunovitz, the family doctor. Anders was transported to the doctor's office, where Dr. Dunovitz picked all of the bark out of his arm and hand. Anders was assured that he had no fractures and would heal in a few weeks.

And he did.

Many years later, as Anders rafted down the Grand Canyon on the Colorado with a group of friends through enormous rapids, he remembered that scary Sunday afternoon on the north fork of the American River.

FIVE

The "Vounded Bird"

Winter in Auburn was greeted with anticipation. Although Anders failed to learn enough Norwegian to speak fluently, his father's Norwegian heritage was enough to ensure that he was included in the inner circle of skiers.

The small, tight-knit Norwegian community in Auburn had an inordinate influence on the social life of the town. Since their arrival to work in the lumber industry, their proficiency on the ski hills had created an enormous amount of excitement and had stimulated the formation of a ski club. Most of the town's kids had taken up skiing, and when Roy Mickelson won the national jumping championship Auburn was finally on the map. In the late fall after trout season was over and the snow began to pile up in the Sierras, a migration up the highway toward Donner Summit occurred every weekend. Skiing suddenly was more popular than football, basketball, or baseball and the members of the high school ski team wore their letter sweaters with great pride.

Roy Mickelson and several of his Norwegian friends, one of whom won the national cross-country championship, spent time each weekend teaching the fine points of ski racing to the locals. Because the most important event to Roy Mickelson was ski jumping, this received special emphasis. Week after week Anders and his friends worked hard packing the snow on the jumping hill and then, under the watchful eye of Roy Mickelson, practiced jumps. Because there were no lifts, after each jump everyone would take off his seven-foot-long skis, trudge back up the hill, and wait his next turn as the Norwegian expert shouted advice. Before the day was over everyone would be exhausted, but if someone had made a jump that warranted praise by Roy it was worth the hard work, cold weather, and repeated tough climbs back up to the in-run of the jump.

The hard work paid off. Boys from Auburn's ski club and high school ski team came home from junior ski meets with many medals and, each time they won, the whole town would celebrate. Although Anders, now fourteen years old, skied well enough to make the team and occasionally won medals in the slalom and downhill, he was a disappointment to Roy on the jumping hill. Late one day after one of his best jumps of about 140 feet, he was elated. He thought he had really "scored." He knew he would finally be one of the anointed. As he trudged back up the hill and approached Roy he heard this comment, "Anders, you yump like a vounded bird." The steadiness in the air during a jump was considered very desirable and points were awarded on form as well as on distance. This was a rebuke he never forgot. It was an epitaph he would always remember with disappointment.

Later, however, Roy laughed and reminded him that it was better to be only wounded as compared to not being able to fly at all. This little bit of wisdom had a lasting effect on Anders. He realized that being part of the team was a small victory and a whole lot better than never getting into the action at all. Many times the memory of Roy's remark that being wounded was better than not flying seemed to reassure Anders that one had to learn to deal with disappointments.

Anders' high school skiing competition turned into an asset

after he entered UC Berkeley. He was offered a job during the five-week Christmas break as a ski host at Badger Pass, the ski center of Yosemite Valley. There he acted as a guide for guests who were unfamiliar with the mountain and had great fun mixing with many of the celebrities that frequented Badger Pass and the Ahwahnee Hotel.

— SIX —

CAMP PAHATSI

I n Auburn in the thirties many children were expected to be responsible in their early teens, far beyond the expectations practiced today. Anders' parents were no exception in these expectations.

Melvin, Anders' father, along with other parents, helped alter a large lodge in the High Sierras that had been purchased from a group of Chinese who claimed their parents built it in the late 1800s. The lodge was on the shores of a small lake about five miles from Soda Springs, California. It had been originally planned as a summer camp, and even before Anders was old enough to be a scout he spent several weeks there in the summer while his father and others from Auburn worked on the lodge and the surrounding facilities. It was a beautiful spot surrounded by enormous pines, firs, and mountain alder.

After a few years it was decided that the lodge should be used as a base for winter skiing as well. About half a mile north of the lodge, the Southern Pacific Railway ran from Sacramento toward its crossing at Donner Summit, about fifteen miles to the east. Nearly 1,000 feet below the railroad ran Highway 40 (now Highway 80), the only road kept open during the winter between California and Nevada near Lake Tahoe.

Because of the heavy winter snowfalls, much of the railroad right-of-way in this region was covered by snowsheds. However, a half-mile stretch near the scout camp was uncovered.

During the winter of 1935 the snow at Pahatsi was about twenty feet deep, and in preparation for the skiing season the lodge had been stocked with provisions with plenty of firewood stored in a large woodshed next door.

The five-mile cross-country skiing from Soda Springs to the lodge was a real adventure and Anders, now fourteen years old, and his four friends were excited as they skied this path through the heavy snow.

A few weeks before, the scoutmaster had arranged for a friend to bring a scout troop of about twenty boys from Marin County, just north of San Francisco, for a four-day stay at the lodge. They were to come on the train that would stop and allow them to unload near the lodge. The Auburn scoutmaster had recruited the five "older" scouts to go with him the day before to open the lodge and meet their city friends at the train, to lead them to the lodge and help with the cooking and the ski equipment.

The day Anders and the boys were to leave Auburn, the scoutmaster called Anders' father and said that due to an emergency he had been unable to get away until the next day and requested that Melvin accompany the boys on the trip. Melvin was also unable to go and after some discussion they decided that Anders should go with the four other boys and take care of things, as he had been to the lodge a number of times before. He would meet their guests the next afternoon.

Anders was the oldest of the five and had earlier been designated as senior patrol leader of the scout troop and, therefore, was in charge of the excursion. A real surge of excitement rippled through the five boys as they realized here was a chance for a real adventure without any adults.

At 3 p.m. the following day it started to snow, but there was no wind and Anders had no concern that it would hamper their plans as they hauled the two toboggans out to the track. At 4 p.m., right on schedule, the Southern Pacific train came into view and ground to a halt. Amid shouting and much excitement all the scouts and their scoutmaster, Mr. Tidwell, a balding, pudgy man, disembarked. They loaded their gear onto the toboggans as the train whistled and pulled away, leaving all the boys waving goodbye. It promised to be a wonderful excursion.

None of the group from Marin had skis, and as they started back toward the lodge they were sinking almost up to their hips in the snow. The going was really tough and complicated by the altitude, which was 7,000 feet. As the boys forged ahead Anders stayed back with the scoutmaster, who was obviously laboring to make it through the deep snow. Less than 100 yards from the railroad track, Mr. Tidwell suddenly pitched forward into the snow.

A sense of helplessness surged over Anders as he shouted for help, threw off his skis, and pulled Mr. Tidwell's pack off his back and rolled him over. His face was blue and he was making an awful gurgling sound. (This was about thirty years before CPR had been developed.) Nothing in his Boy Scout training or first-aid manual had prepared Anders or the other boys for this event. Within a minute or two Mr. Tidwell stopped making any noise and no longer appeared to be breathing. By this time most of the troop had returned to the scene and some started crying. It suddenly dawned on Anders that he was in charge and had to do something. He thought Mr. Tidwell might be dead but he certainly wasn't sure. There were no adults to help him or to tell him what to do or to confirm the diagnosis.

Anders decided to send everyone on to the lodge except his friend Richard, who was also an excellent skier. The boys thought that if Mr. Tidwell were alive, he needed medical attention fast! They would try to get him down to the highway. Just across the track, the mountain dropped away in a very steep slope for about 600 or 700 feet and over a mile to the road. That was their only chance to get help.

Anders and Richard put Mr. Tidwell in his sleeping bag and roped him onto the toboggan. After dragging him across the tracks they started down the mountain. Richard skied in front and Anders skied in the back to act as a brake, which would control their downhill speed. The first 200 yards were okay, but it was beginning to get dark and the fear caused their hearts to pound. In spite of the freezing cold, they began to sweat profusely.

As the slope got steeper, Anders was having more and more trouble holding the toboggan back as he snowplowed for dear life. They got going faster and faster and suddenly Anders pitched forward on his face in the snow. He lost hold of the rope to the toboggan, and Mr. Tidwell and the toboggan went charging past Richard and down the mountain through the trees and out of sight.

Now, as the two boys stared down the mountain, guilt became more powerful than fear. Fortunately, the tracks in the new fallen snow were easy to follow and even in the evening dusk and after about ten minutes they found their man still roped to the toboggan but upside down in a snowbank. He had hurdled over a steep bank and landed upside down and was almost buried. They rushed to the toboggan, rolled it over, and brushed the snow from his face. In the fading light they convinced themselves that if he had not been dead when they started down the mountain, then they had killed him for sure.

The boys sat in the snow for a while fighting back the tears and assessing their next move. They soon promised each other that no one would ever know about the escaped toboggan. The remaining 400 feet down, over possibly 1,000 yards, was very steep, so they waded through the snow on foot with the toboggan and Mr. Tidwell on a towrope. By the time they reached the road (then Highway 40), they were cold and exhausted and it was dark.

They lowered Mr. Tidwell down onto the snowbank, which had been cut by a snowplow, and waited for a car. About four or five cars heading down the grade passed without stopping, in spite of their wild hollering and waving. Soon, however, a man passed but then stopped and backed up and focused his headlights on the toboggan and Mr. Tidwell's frozen face. When he got out of his car and took a look, he got a panic-stricken expression. He didn't say a word, but jumped into his car and drove off into the night.

The boys were so cold and frightened they wanted to cry. A few minutes later, however, a truck coming up the grade stopped, and when the driver saw their plight, helped load Mr. Tidwell into the back of his truck. He squeezed both boys into the cab, and as they chugged up the grade he listened to their story. They told him everything except about the escaped toboggan. After about two miles, the driver found a place to turn around and they headed down the grade in what was now a blinding blizzard.

About an hour later they pulled into the little town of Colfax, where they located a doctor, who pronounced Mr. Tidwell dead. The doctor then recorded their account of the event and insisted the two boys sign his notes. He then called Anders' family in Auburn, about twenty miles down the road.

A short time afterward, Anders' father arrived to further interrogate the boys on the events of the day. They drove home, where a warm house and hot meal were waiting. Anders' mother lectured Melvin for letting the boys go up there without an adult. Melvin called Pahatsi and, luckily, the phone was working. The boys were warm and well fed but very worried about their scoutmaster. A fair amount of tears were shed when they heard the news.

By the next morning the snow had stopped and Melvin and scoutmaster Mr. Tobias, Richard, and Anders drove back to Soda Springs and spent the next three days trying to make the trip a worthwhile experience for their guests. At the end of the three days, as the boys from Marin County boarded the train for the return trip home, there was no whooping and hollering. They were a sober group heading home from a mountain adventure they would never forget. It was also a trip Richard and Anders would always remember, and although they talked about it occasionally, for many years they did not divulge that the toboggan had gotten away. Never was there a time, however, whether summer or winter, that the boys remembered Pahatsi without suffering from a sense of uneasiness and guilt.

For many years thereafter Pahatsi served as a scout camp in the summer and a ski resort in the winter—until the summer of 2003, when it suddenly burned down.

SEVEN

RED'S RHYTHM RASCALS

The piano lessons by Mrs. Warren were typical of those given to children whom everyone hoped would become classical virtuosos. Anders was at first lukewarm about the process and the obligated one hour of practice a day. Plus, for Anders the concentration on scales and other techniques failed to produce what sounded like music. After about a year, however, when he became more interested in the music of Bach, Beethoven, Mozart, and Brahms it began to seem like the practice was really worth the effort. Lessons and practice continued until Anders reached age thirteen, when he started playing trumpet in the high school band and as modern music, from such greats as Tommy Dorsey, Glenn Miller, and the like, sounded more fun than the old masters. Because the high school bandmaster needed a trombonist more than a trumpet player, Anders switched brass instruments and began to see himself as a versatile musician.

One evening after a high school concert when Anders was fifteen years old, a stranger approached and wanted to know if he would like to try out for a dance band called "Red's Rhythm Rascals." Red Berman, who was redheaded but almost bald and seemed like a good guy, explained that he was the leader of the band and also its drummer. It sounded exciting, and shortly thereafter Anders was playing with an eight-piece band that performed at school dances, grange hall dances, special parties, and, most fun of all, the Annual Frog Jump of Calaveras County at Angel's Camp.

Angel's Camp was an old mining town about fifty miles south of Auburn. The musicians were often paid ten dollars for a night's work, which, compared to the eighteen cents an hour Anders earned picking pears in the summer, seemed like a windfall. Even more important, standing in front of the band with the spotlight in his eyes, playing a trombone solo, insured a minor celebrity status, even in 1937 and 1938. The cute girls who did the vocals were also an attraction.

The third weekend in August was the most fun, as the annual frog jump, popularized by the chronicles of life in the mother lode, described by Mark Twain, was an exciting event. *The Celebrated Jumping Frog of Calaveras County* had been reenacted annually for many years and attracted large crowds, who always seemed to be in a party mood. The dance lasted until 2 a.m., after which the musicians loaded their instruments into their cars and headed home for Auburn. Red and the sax player were in the front seat and Anders and Suzie, a vivacious little blond vocalist, were in the back. After about half an hour, as the car wound through the mountain roads, Suzie and Anders became involved in some necking, which was ignored completely by those in the front seat.

All of a sudden Suzie stiffened and started convulsing. Anders was terrified. He didn't know if it was his fault or what to do. Suzie's teeth clamped shut on her tongue, which started to bleed. Anders shouted, "Stop the car, Red," which brought the response, "Anders, what did you do to her?" No one knew what to do so they opened the car door and dragged her out onto the roadside, where she continued to seizure for what seemed like forever. Anders wished Max Dunovitz was available, as he would know what to do. Finally, Suzie stopped convulsing and lay unconscious in the grass while the guys dabbed her head with cold water from a nearby stream and wished they had some knowledge of how to treat convulsions. They were in a remote mountain valley about twenty miles from Auburn at 3 a.m. There was no way to communicate with anyone.

After some time she opened her eyes, looked at her companions, and started to cry. She sobbed and sobbed and explained that she was an epileptic, but up to now no one outside of her family had known. She said that she had been through these spells a number of times and was so embarrassed she could hardly stop sobbing.

When she was finally delivered home to her family at about 4 a.m., her parents blamed the bandleader for her attack, saying that the late hours were certainly the cause. Anders was somewhat relieved that her mother didn't blame him. Thereafter, Anders decided that romance with a vocalist was fraught with more complications than he was ready for. In the years following, he always had a slight aversion to cute little vocalists who everyone else thought were so darling. Suzie gave up singing with the band and, as far as anyone knew, was able to prevent further seizures by getting to bed early and avoiding amorous necking parties. Red's Rhythm Rascals continued to perform but without a vocalist, and even after Anders went off to the University of California, Berkeley, he would occasionally play with them when home on vacation.

So much for Anders' career as a professional musician. Years later, in medical school, he would describe his experience to the chief of neurology, who used the story as a case to illustrate the management of epilepsy.

EIGHT

THE ERICKSSEN LINEAGE

Anders' father, Melvin, had come west from rural Minnesota, a center for Norwegian immigrants. His parents arrived in the U.S. on a ship late in the 1800s and settled in Minnesota in a small town, East Grand Forks, where Norwegian was the most common language. As a child he went to a Norwegian grammar school for four years and then learned how to be a farmhand with his older brother, Theodore, and younger brother, John, and worked along with the other farmhands on his father's farm. Although he learned to speak some English he was more comfortable speaking Norwegian, which the farmhands used exclusively. Like many Norwegian farmers, Melvin's father, Andrew, often drank heavily on weekends and was frequently abusive to Melvin's mother. During one of his parents' altercations, Melvin came to his mother's defense. The ensuing fistfight with his father resulted in Melvin's being badly beaten and ejected from the family. Here he was, a thirteen-year-old Norwegian boy with limited English, rejected by his family, and, as such, ostracized by the whole Norwegian community. What would he do?

Melvin had heard stories about a Norwegian farmer in Oregon who hired Norwegian farmhands. By age thirteen he had become an experienced farmer, so he jumped on a freight train headed west, eventually arriving in Oregon, where he was hired as a farm-hand and worked at this job for several years. When he was nineteen years old his expectations were abruptly altered.

About that time, the local neighborhood one-room school hired a new teacher, Myrtle Dunton, who had grown up in Richmond, California, where her father had managed a brickyard. She had qualified as a teacher by attending a "normal school." These schools were two-year teachers' colleges, and at the turn of the century were the standard way to become a schoolteacher.

Melvin immediately fell in love with this girl from California but knew she was much better educated than he, and, having had no significant education, it suddenly became clear how limited he was.

Although he had attended only four years of a Norwegian grammar school, he somehow managed to be admitted to Oregon State University. How this happened was always a family mystery. He worked to support himself as he went to college, and occasionally he would return to Central Point to visit Myrtle, whom he was determined to marry when he became educated. Although she had been courted by some of the affluent young farmers in the area, she decided to wait for Melvin. Just as he was graduating with a teacher's credential, World War I started and Melvin joined the army, so that after a nine-year courtship and discharge from the army the couple was finally married.

When he was offered a teaching job in Auburn, California, where he knew there was a small Norwegian colony, he jumped at the chance. Myrtle was also glad to return to California, where they could occasionally visit her parents who had subsequently moved to Santa Maria.

As Anders grew up in Auburn, the story of his father's struggles as a child were held up as proof that one could succeed, provided he was willing to exert enough energy and determination. Melvin lived the kind of life he preached. Every hour that he was not teaching he occupied himself with jobs, including repairing school buses, building rental houses, repairing old cars, and working in the church with the Boy Scouts and other civic activities. As Anders went through high school it was made clear that his behavior had to reflect credit on his father, who was on the faculty. At one time Anders got a C in Latin. The Latin teacher explained to Melvin that she didn't think Anders was college material. That night was a tumultuous one in the Erickssen household. Melvin was furious. He explained to Anders how embarrassed he was that a teacher would have this impression of his son, and Anders' driving privileges were terminated for one semester. Never again did Anders dare to get a C.

Anders' parents also made it clear that although they would help him in college he should plan to pay his own way as far as possible. It turned out to be possible. Tuition at Cal was fifteen dollars a semester and jobs were available on campus at Berkeley and in the industries around the campus. Besides doing dishes at the Theta Chi house, Anders worked in the University Extension division, in a local foundry, and finally in the Richmond shipyard. This resulted in his having a little nest egg when he finally went away to medical school.

Melvin enjoyed his relationship with Anders, was extremely proud of Anders' achievements, but also made it clear that he believed hard work and persistence would "get Anders farther than being a smart aleck and tooting his own horn." Melvin also preached that listening would get you farther than talking.

– NINE –

SMOKE RINGS IN BERKELEY

In his senior year of high school many discussions about college with Dr. Max Dunowitz and others convinced Anders that the University of California at Berkeley was the ideal choice. Its academic standards were unparalleled and the tuition was very low.

When Anders arrived at the UC campus in Berkeley it was somewhat of a culture shock. In Auburn, a city of 2,000, he knew everyone in town. The undergraduate enrollment at UC was 18,000 and he knew only one person—Professor Hildebrand, who was head of the chemistry department and coach of the Cal ski team. Anders had met Dr. Hildebrand at many ski meets and felt that when he had a problem he would always have someone to go to for advice.

After a few visits to several fraternities he joined Theta Chi, mainly because they had an attractive chapter house close to the campus and because they offered him a job washing dishes, which would pay his monthly house bill of eighty dollars. Most of the students in the fraternity were from the San Francisco Bay area but a couple were from Southern California, a place, according to Berkeley standards, where mostly "weirdos" lived.

Within a few weeks Anders had some good friends, especially

his roommate Hilary Crawford, son of a prominent attorney in San Francisco. The social event of each day was the evening meal around a large oval table where jokes, stories, and talk of the sports teams dominated. Friday night was special, as it was the time when most of the fraternity members finished the meal by smoking cigars. Anders didn't smoke, but because he was always waiting on tables and washing dishes it wasn't so obvious. After a few months, as in most groups, a sort of pecking order developed. Because Anders was from a small town and most of the other members were from the city, and also because he worked in the kitchen, he was near the bottom of this hierarchy. The fact that he had gone out for the boxing team, however, was the one status symbol he had in his favor. Several of the boys from San Francisco started calling him "country boy," which was definitely not a term of endearment.

He was beginning to get used to studying much harder than he ever had in Auburn, especially enjoying organic chemistry. This was not only because he was doing well in chemistry but also because he was very attracted to his lab partner, Sarah Birnbaum. She was a very bright, vivacious brunette who not only enjoyed the experiments in the lab three days a week but also the evenings when they studied chemistry together in the library or her dormitory.

When football season started it seemed like college life was going well for Anders. The evenings after a football game the girl-friends were invited to share hot chocolate around the enormous fireplace at the fraternity and sing college songs. During this time, in the 1940s, no alcohol was allowed on campus. After a few weeks Anders invited Sarah to join him at a party, and when he delivered her home to the dormitory afterward he decided that, despite that some guys called him "country boy," life at Berkeley was going fine. When he returned back to the chapter house the girls had all been taken home and most of the members were sitting around discussing life and the fact that the football team had won over Oregon that day.

When Anders came in, Bruno Corielle, a senior pre-law student from San Francisco, who had anointed Anders with the name "country boy," stood up and in a loud voice said, "What do you know, country boy likes kikes. What does her father do, Anders? Is he a tailor or does he sell shoes? You will soon learn we don't like kikes in our fraternity house."

Anders was floored. It had never even occurred to him that she was Jewish. As far as he knew, he had never met anyone who was anti-Semitic and here was one of the most influential upperclassmen in the fraternity telling Anders his girlfriend wasn't welcome. He was furious. Dr. Dunovitz, one of the people he admired most in the world, was Jewish. As he looked around the room he saw no sympathetic faces and decided not to debate the issue. He withdrew to his room and fumed. How many of the other chapter members agreed with Corielle? He couldn't be sure.

As the weeks went on, it became apparent that a low-grade anti-Semitism was common all over the Berkeley campus though mostly concentrated in the fraternities. Anders agonized over the event but was especially disappointed when his best friend, Hilary Crawford, counseled him to get used to it. "It's no big deal." From that day on Anders accepted living in this bigoted environment, especially because his job in the kitchen paid his way and most of his fraternity brothers seemed to genuinely like him. Corielle was another matter. Anders' distaste for him continued to grow.

One Friday evening as Anders was cleaning the table and cigar smoke was fairly thick, Corielle blew smoke rings at Anders and sneered, "Can you do that, country boy?" Anders seethed. He blurted out, "Any half-brained chimpanzee can do that." Corielle smiled and replied, "Five bucks says you can't do it." Anders was working his way through Cal and five bucks was a lot of money to him. How to save face in this very embarrassing situation? He finally said, "Give me one week, I'll blow smoke rings. I'll take your bet." Several of his fraternity brothers wanted to get in on the bet. Anders was really worried that he had bitten off more than he could chew.

He retired to his room to discuss his plight with Hilary, his roommate, who smoked cigars and was very good at blowing smoke rings. Hilary said, "I think you can do it, but cigar smoke is essential. We need a lot of cigars." Off they went to the corner cigar store and bought about thirty of the cheapest cigars available. And so the smoke ring lessons began. After about half an hour of puffing cigars, Anders began to get nauseated. Sometimes he would actually vomit. Hilary kept encouraging him, explaining how to hold his mouth and tongue as he exhaled the noxious smoke. After several days he began to make a few rings and by the next Friday he was ready, although he had spent almost the whole week sick to his stomach. After he had picked up the dishes, he entered the dining room. He sat down next to Corielle, lifted a cigar and blew smoke rings in Corielle's face. All of his fraternity brothers cheered as he collected his five dollars. His social status was suddenly elevated, and he was labeled a real winner. Hilary was especially proud, as he also had a low opinion of Corielle. At this point the "country boy" had almost become a sophisticated college man.

If ever there had been a chance that Anders might become a smoker, that week learning to blow smoke rings was the coup de grace.

– TEN –

THE WINTER OF '41

Life at the Theta Chi fraternity had settled into a routine. Keeping up with the academic pressure was new for Anders, who had previously had no trouble in this regard. Grades on each exam were scored on a "curve," so if you were in a class with high achievers you could get an eighty-five on an exam and get a C or a ninety-five and get a B. It seemed to Anders that everyone at Berkeley was an academic achiever, so that keeping up his grades was a major challenge, one that he had never really faced before.

Although he was not doing as well scholastically as he had hoped, Anders enjoyed many of his classmates as well as the intellectual interchange. He also met some very attractive girls besides Sarah Birnbaum, including Helen Crawford, the sister of his roommate Hilary. One of his best friends was a recent immigrant from Poland who with his family had barely escaped Hitler's slaughter. Jerczy Spitzer was a short, stocky fellow who was a very serious student and told Anders many stories about Nazi atrocities in Poland. Anders also kept in touch with the professor of the chemistry department, Dr. Hildebrand, who, as noted, was the coach of the Cal Ski Team and whom Anders had met many times in years past when competing in high school ski meets, which had attracted college ski coaches.

Early in November Dr. Hildebrand called Anders and invited him to work at Badger Pass, the ski resort in Yosemite Valley, during the Christmas vacation. It sounded like a wonderful opportunity and turned out that there would also be an opening for Anders' friend Jerczy Spitzer, who had learned to ski as a child in Europe. Anders spent a number of hours telling Jerczy about Badger Pass and Yosemite, describing the beautiful Ahwahnee Hotel in anticipation of the fun in the snow where they would work as hosts, guiding visitors around the valley and to the appropriate best ski runs during the Christmas vacation.

Semester final exams at Cal were starting on December 8, 1941, and one week later the young men would leave for what promised to be a wonderful Christmas break. Sunday morning, December 7th, Anders was up early serving breakfast in the fraternity and finishing the dishes and then retired to his room to start cramming for the exams that would begin the next day. About two hours into this study session, Hilary, his roommate, opened the door and shouted "The Japs have bombed Pearl Harbor. We are at war."

Anders was shocked. "Where is Pearl Harbor?" he exclaimed.

"It's in Hawaii," Hilary retorted. "They may bomb San Francisco and Berkeley today. Who knows?"

The rest of the day Berkeley was in bedlam. From the campus one could see San Francisco Bay and the Golden Gate Bridge, and everyone half expected to see squadrons of Japanese bombers honing in on the Cal campus. Hardly anyone continued to study.

Monday morning found Anders and his classmates bleary-eyed from bull sessions almost all night, struggling with the semester final exams. The rest of the week, most of the pre-med students in Anders' class tried to ignore the war hysteria and concentrate on their examinations. Friday afternoon the exams were over, and without any feedback on the results Anders and Jerczy boarded a bus for Yosemite Valley, which delivered them at Badger Pass long after midnight.

The next morning was a beautiful day. The two young men were issued camp parkas with a Yosemite logo, introduced to the other employees, and given a lecture by the chief of the ski school, Luggi Foeger. Luggi was an Austrian professional who had become famous for his wins in a number of international downhill races, as well as excelling in jumping in his youth. This was followed by half a day of free skiing, which helped them become more familiar with the various runs and the main lift, a large sled pulled up by a cable powered by a gas engine. This was before there were chair lifts at Yosemite. Chair lifts had just been introduced by Averell Harriman at Sun Valley, who had designed them after observing buckets carrying ore from a mine in the mountains of Bolivia.

The next day Anders and Jerczy woke up early to one of the heaviest snowfalls they had ever experienced. The snowflakes seemed as big as handkerchiefs. By noon the ground and the lodge roof had two feet of snow and the Badger Pass boys, as Anders and Jerczy became known, were sent up on the roof to shovel snow. For days the snow never stopped and finally accumulated a total of eight feet on the level, which required that every two or three hours, night and day, someone had to go up on the roof and shovel.

The deep snow closed the road from the valley up to Badger Pass, so there were no guests skiing. The lodge employees, when they weren't shoveling snow, were urged to ski down the runs so as to pack them down. Snowmobile tractors that now smooth the runs at virtually all ski resorts were unheard of in 1941. It was great fun. The Japanese and the war seemed worlds away. After four days the snow stopped, the glorious sun came out, and the following day the snowplows opened the road and the skiers returned.

For the next three weeks between snowfalls and bouts of shoveling, Anders and Jerczy skied, visited with hotel guests, and led them down their favorite runs. In the evenings, after the guests had left Badger Pass to return to the Ahwahnee Hotel, Jerczy described in detail his awful experiences in Poland. He reiterated how he and his family had fled down a country road, hiding in ditches as the Nazi Messerschmitts strafed and bombed the helpless refugees. Jerczy and his family had been living in Krakow and were hoping to get to the coast, where they had been promised a boat ride to St. Petersburg. There they had hoped to eventually ride trains full of refugees across Siberia; then, when they arrived at the Pacific Coast, they would catch a ship to Seattle.

Jerczy said it was a miracle that he and his father and mother, carrying all their worldly goods on their backs, had escaped the daily strafing. The memories of struggling past those who had been hit by machine gun fire and lay dead or dying or of running with crowds of others diving into the ditches along the side of the road when they heard the planes coming would be imprinted on his brain forever. He said, "Can you believe that Neville Chamberlain, Prime Minister of England, had just signed a peace treaty with Hitler and announced to the world 'There will be peace in our time'? All the time Hitler was murdering innocent Jews and Poles by the thousands."

That winter, the days and nights flew by. As Anders heard Jerczy's stories his admiration for Jerczy and those who were finally going to war against Hitler became an emotion that would linger for the rest of his life. Never would Anders be able to be a pacifist.

One day Anders was assigned to guide a party of four on an overnight trip to Ostrander Lake, about seven miles away. The Camp Curry Company maintained a beautiful lodge there, where you could ski, spend the night, and be served a sumptuous banquet and then ski back to Badger Pass the next day. He always enjoyed these trips because he had a chance to visit with the guests both on the trip and during the evening meal.

This morning, when he was introduced to his guests, he immediately recognized Claudette Colbert, a very popular French movie actress, who was also an excellent skier. Her husband—a doctor—and the other couple were also good skiers and very friendly. On that evening at Ostrander Lodge they regaled Anders with stories about skiing in Switzerland and France. Claudette kidded Anders with the comment that she was always crazy about Norwegian skiers. That night, Anders decided that someday he too would ski in Switzerland and France. He also fantasized about marrying a beautiful movie star.

The next day was exciting, as Anders described to Jerczy his experience with this famous movie actress and her friends. It would also be a great story to tell at the Theta Chi house when he returned to Berkeley.

Not surprisingly, when Anders returned to school he found that almost everyone's grades had slipped a little since December 7th, as well as their confidence that they would be able to pursue their college education. Within a few weeks a military draft was established and several special programs were instituted on campus to encourage voluntary enlistment into the armed forces. Anders and most of the pre-med students signed up for either the Army or Navy Reserve Program. These programs offered the chance to finish college and then be obligated after graduation to attend a three-month training to become an officer. These officers were dubbed "ninety-day wonders." Anders signed up to be in the Navy's reserve program. He was told that if upon graduation he had been admitted to medical school he would be allowed to continue school as an active member of the Naval Reserve. It certainly seemed like a better deal than becoming a ninety-day wonder with an assignment to a destroyer as an Ensign Gunnery Officer!

The ski team was disbanded along with many of the other activities on campus. A few of Anders' close Japanese friends were sent to the internment camps at Tulle Lake. In Auburn, all was not well. Of course, Germany had invaded Norway, an especially dastardly act, according to Anders' father, who reminded Anders that the Swedes had allowed the Germans to occupy their country without a fight. When the Japanese farmers who lived around Auburn were evacuated to Tulle Lake, Anders' father and another schoolteacher formed a partnership to try to find renters for their farms. Melvin was convinced that the local Japanese farmers were loyal Americans who offered no threat to the U.S. and were being treated very badly. He also found storage for some of their cars and trucks. Most people in Auburn, however, weren't happy with Melvin's activities. Melvin repeatedly complained to Anders that he was receiving a number of threats and that there was a group moving to try to get him fired from his job at the high school. It was a tumultuous time. As the anti-Japanese sentiment escalated, Anders worried about his father's welfare.

By June of 1942 the new Kaiser shipyards in Richmond, California, had been established. They planned to build liberty ships on an assembly line basis, almost like cars. They established a student swing shift, which Anders joined. He could finish his classes by 2 p.m., get on a bus to Richmond, finish his shift by 11 p.m., and be back in Berkeley by midnight. His final year at Berkeley was very busy. Somehow he managed forty hours a week at the Kaiser shipyard, working as a stage rigger, and taking eighteen units at Cal. A stage rigger built scaffolds up the sides of the ships' hulls that allowed the riveters to work on the ships' forty or fifty feet up the side of the hull.

He graduated with a degree, an admission to medical school, and the rank of Apprentice Seaman in the Navy (the lowest rank possible). This rank he would carry all through medical school. With the war raging on two fronts, Apprentice Seaman Anders Erickssen headed off to medical school in Louisville, Kentucky.

As Anders left to go to Louisville, he and Jerczy met one last time. Jerczy Spitzer had graduated in chemistry with honors and had enlisted in the Army. He explained that the enlistment would automatically give him U.S. citizenship. "I'm so lucky, to finally be a citizen of the most wonderful country in the world." As he made this statement, tears ran down his cheeks. Anders realized he was also crying as they embraced for the last time. About a year later, when Anders was in Louisville Medical School, he got a letter from Jerczy's mother. Jerczy had been killed by a German mortar the day before the Germans surrendered. Anders was crushed and somehow felt guilty. How could this wonderful patriotic immigrant be killed while here Anders was safe in medical school?

Thirty years later as Anders stood on the veranda of a lodge in Zermatt and viewed the Matterhorn for the first time, his memories of the stories told by Claudette Colbert and of his experiences with Jerczy Spitzer came back in vivid detail.

ELEVEN

THE UNIVERSITY OF LOUISVILLE

It was 6 a.m. when Anders disembarked from the train in Louisville, Kentucky. The still gray sky looked cold, as indeed it was. A light snow was falling but, unlike the snow in California, it was gray, and intermingled in the snowflakes were particles of soot that, when they landed on a white shirt, left a tell-tale mark. Anders had made a reservation at the Brown Hotel, in the middle of the city, where he would stay until he found a permanent residence. After depositing his two suitcases and having a southern breakfast of ham hocks, eggs, and biscuits, he decided to walk through the city to the medical school, which was about a mile away, according to the people in the hotel. He wanted to look around and eventually register.

Even though he had his warmest overcoat and ski gloves, he shivered a little as he plodded through a few inches of gray snow on the sidewalk. His first impression of Louisville was not too positive; everything was gray due to the universal use of soft coal for heating, electrical power, and conventional manufacturing. When he arrived at the medical school, the sight was startling. The four-story stone building, with a broad front staircase leading up to an elevated main floor, looked like an old castle. For a Californian, where almost all the buildings were relatively new, this 100-year-old edifice was a novel experience. Inside, however, it was warm and inviting as he joined a crowd of students milling around, sharing their first impressions of the institution that was to launch them on their life's quest.

A very friendly fellow, Jim Appleton, approached Anders and introduced himself. "I'm from Ohio. Where are you from? California? I thought you had sort of a funny accent. Do you have a place to live yet? No? Then let's find a place together. We can be roommates." Jim's outgoing, friendly manner and Midwest drawl appealed to Anders, and he knew he had found a new friend. Soon after they finished their formal registration they met Gene Combs, who was from the AKK fraternity, looking to find freshmen to help fill his fraternity house, which would help pay the bills.

Anders, like many of his classmates, was in the Naval Reserve, which would soon place him on active duty in medical school and pay for his lodging and tuition. Jim and Anders decided that Gene, who had a pronounced Southern accent, seemed like a very nice guy, so they both walked to the fraternity house, which was about four blocks from school. This area of Louisville was a run-down ghetto, housing mostly Negroes, as they were referred to in 1943. The old house had undoubtedly been a Southern mansion maybe 100 years ago but looked pretty shabby compared to the Theta Chi house in Berkeley, which Anders had just left. They were introduced to Louie and Edward, the cook and the houseboy, and soon were settled in what for the next two years was to be their room on the third floor.

The first day of school was a little unsettling when the dean, after welcoming the new students to the university, announced, "Look around at your classmates. One out of four will be gone next year. We have one hundred in our freshman class but only room for seventy-five next year. Your grades and class standings will be posted after each examination as a stimulus to encourage scholarship. Those who fail will probably be sent to active duty in the Pacific Theater." A rather disturbing statement. The stories about the war against Japan at that time were grim.

The next day in the anatomy lab, Jim and Anders were introduced to their cadaver. Dead Ernestine would be their companion for a year as they carefully dissected her from skin to bones. As the year went on they became quite attached to Ernestine, as did most of the students to the body that would have the greatest impact on their experience during their whole medical curriculum.

Medical school at Louisville in 1943 was more clinically oriented than in later years. Although the courses in pathology, physiology, bacteriology, and pharmacology introduced the students to the knowledge base of the time, each contained information on how important basic science was in understanding what was known about the diseases that were common then. Special emphasis was placed on endemic tuberculosis and syphilis, while rheumatic fever was about the only process that occupied those who were interested in the heart. Heart attacks were of secondary interest.

Anders and Jim had no trouble with the year-end cut but felt very bad for those who knew that they were on the verge of leaving a program they had pointed to for years, especially with the thought that they probably had to go to war against the Japanese. As time passed, studying became a routine on weeknights and parties, often with too much bourbon, occupied the weekends.

Jim and Anders bought two bicycles and a Model T Ford for twenty-five dollars and learned to repair it when it broke down, which was frequent. This contributed to their reputation as being slightly eccentric, a characteristic they both relished. Along with a medical education Anders was obligated to learn a little about the Navy, as the Navy Department was paying his tuition, board, and room. He continued to have the rank of Apprentice Seaman and each Saturday morning was required to listen to lectures about naval strategy.

TWELVE

CARING FOR PATIENTS

The third year in medical school is probably the most exciting for students. The academic grind of getting through the basic sciences necessary to practice medicine is behind and the student actually starts examining and treating patients. The first rotation for Anders was OB (obstetrics).

He started out as an assistant to one of the junior faculty members, scrubbing in for deliveries, and within a few weeks had actually delivered a baby, tied off the cord, and sewed up the episiotomy. At the end of the third month of OB he was assigned to a home delivery three-person team consisting of a senior medical student, an OB nurse, and himself. Almost all the mothers assigned to the home delivery service were multips, mothers who had already had several babies.

On the first few trips he assisted the senior medical student with the delivery, both of them under the watchful eye of the nurse, who had been on this service for years and probably could have done the delivery without help. Anders' job as an assistant consisted mainly of giving a little light anesthesia by dripping ether onto a mask covering the mother's nose and mouth. This experience provided him an inside look at the homes where most of the blacks in Louisville lived. Some of the homes were reasonably comfortable but many were without electricity. After two years in Louisville, Anders had become familiar with their special singsongy brand of the Southern accent and felt that he had an affinity with many whom he had administered to.

After about a month had passed and he had assisted about twenty deliveries, his home delivery senior medical student partner announced, "The next run we make you will do the delivery and I will give the anesthetic." Anders really felt he was ready. This was going to be his day to show how well he could do. At about 5:30 p.m. the next day the OB office got the call. Home delivery on Canal Street. During the prenatal visit each mother had drawn a map to show how to get to her home. So, with map in hand, Anders, Howard—Anders' senior partner—and Emily— the OB nurse—loaded the home delivery supplies into their van and headed for Canal Street.

When they arrived in the vicinity described on the map it became apparent that most of the houses were on pilings, to allow for the occasional high water that would come with the winter floods on the Ohio River. With their flashlights, they located a little house on pilings about eight feet above the muddy road where they had parked. They struggled up the ladder with their home delivery equipment and entered a one-room house lit by kerosene lamps. They were met by a jolly, rotund lady, who greeted them with, "Hi, I'm Pearl, Jasmine's mother. You guys got here about the right time."

Jasmine, who appeared to be about sixteen years old, was having her third baby and had been in labor a couple of hours. The four other people in the room appeared to be friends or family members. It was evident they had all been involved in previous home deliveries, and had definite opinions as to how it should be done. An examination revealed that Jasmine was partly dilated, and it seemed as though it would be some time before she would deliver. Howard said, "Anders, it's your show. Take charge and get the baby out of there."

After about half an hour it was quite evident that Pearl, Jasmine's mother, was going to be part of the delivery team. In rapid fire she described the number of deliveries she had been involved in without the help of doctors. Jasmine's cries at each contraction were answered by several people in the room, "Don't cry, baby, you will be okay, we're all here." Although her cervix was now almost completely dilated, she seemed to have stopped bearing down with each pain in spite of Anders' and Pearl's calling out in encouragement.

Suddenly Pearl said, "Doctor, is it time to quill her?" Anders had no idea what she was talking about. Through the gloom he looked at Howard for some help; Howard shrugged—he also had no idea. Anders then glanced at Emily, the nurse, as she was the most experienced. She also shrugged. Anders finally replied, "Not yet." After a few more contractions and groans from Jasmine, Pearl again said "Now can I quill her?" Again Anders, not sure what to say, answered, "Not yet." In a few more minutes Pearl blurted out, "I know it's time to quill her." Anders thought, *Whatever it is, we are not making much progress,* so he said, "Go ahead and quill her." Pearl displayed a long feather, probably from a rooster tail. She carefully threaded it up Jasmine's nose, who responded with a monstrous sneeze, and out popped the baby, who after a slap on the bottom was crying and looked to be doing fine.

And so it was, Anders had learned something about delivering babies that was not in the textbooks. After Anders tied the cord and delivered the placenta, Jasmine seemed fine and was in good spirits holding her new baby and showing him to all the onlookers.

Now it was time to fill out the birth certificate. Anders asked Jasmine each question and wrote her response.

Mother's name? "Jasmine Johnson."

Father's name? "I ain't gonna tell you his father's name. He's a no good nigger. He ain't been around for six months."

Baby's name? "I ain't thought of a name yet. What's your name, Doctor?"

Anders replied, "Doctor Erickssen."

"No, I mean your first name."

"Anders," he muttered.

"Then I'll name him Anders," which after some discussion was entered on the birth certificate.

In later years Anders often wondered what happened to his namesake, a little Negro boy with a Norwegian name. Anders also suggested to his obstetrical friends that they try quilling patients who were slow in labor. This advice, as far as he knew, was never taken.

At the end of each academic year one student would be honored for excellence in Anatomy, Obstetrics, General Surgery, or Psychiatry. Because Anders had taken several psychology courses at Cal and knew all the jargon, each year he was selected for honors in psychiatry. All of his classmates expected that he would become a psychiatrist. During his senior year he was awarded a special assignment of a three-month clerkship in the state's psychiatric hospital. The terrible condition of the patients with central nervous system syphilis, advanced catatonic schizophrenia, and deep depression were so distressing to Anders that he wondered whether he himself would need shock treatment—then a common way to treat the very debilitated psychiatric patients in the state hospital. By the end of the three months, he was convinced that any branch of medicine had to have more appeal than psychiatry.

During his senior year he started dating a cute little Kentucky girl who worked as a secretary in a doctor's office. She was very popular with many of the other medical students and it made Anders feel important that she preferred him to some of his friends who were also interested in her. Near the end of the senior year it seemed like everyone in Anders' class was getting married, so he joined in the fun and married Luci Turner, daughter of a Methodist preacher in a rural town in Kentucky. Months later Anders and Luci headed for Jersey City, where Anders would serve his internship and discover that the heart seemed like an exciting organ to concentrate on.

— THIRTEEN —

THE FIRE

Upon arriving in Jersey City, Luci and Anders found an apartment in a private residence a short bus ride from the medical center. Anders' fifty-dollar-a-month salary would not keep their household going, so Luci found a job in a doctor's office and together they were just barely able to cover their expenses.

The medical center was a 1,200-bed edifice that had been funded by a special grant from the U.S. government. It was rumored to have been a payoff for Mayor Hague's support for Roosevelt when the president had run for his first term. It was a beautiful facility and appeared a little out of place in a city that had a large population of immigrants from Ireland, Poland, Italy, and South America. Politics was very important in social life and there was little doubt that the Irish were in charge and that Mayor Hague was the most important person in the city.

The Jersey City Medical Center internship was rotating. After three months on medicine and one month on general surgery, Anders was assigned to three months at the Margaret Hague Maternity Hospital, where he delivered several babies a day. As the 1st of February rolled around and the coldest weather that had gripped New Jersey and New York for ten years settled in, Anders was assigned to take his turn on the ambulance service. There were two interns and two ambulances, each working for twenty-four hours. Two small bedrooms, a waiting room, and a garage housed the driver and the ambulance, plus the intern. Between calls, which were relayed by the hospital emergency room, the two men could sleep, read, or listen to the radio (this was several years before television). The boys would listen to the ambulance drivers tell tales of their experiences. They were very knowledge-able about medicine in spite of having no formal training. With each call they would listen along with the intern to the patient's complaints and often volunteer their opinion about the diagnosis, what treatment was indicated, and whether the patient should be transported to the hospital. Anders found their homespun brand of medicine humorous but often surprisingly accurate in assess-ment. This was a time when the interns recognized that they were fully in charge and the sense of responsibility was rather exciting.

February 8th had been extraordinarily busy most of the day as Anders and the driver skidded around the icy streets covered with six inches of snow. By 11 p.m. the calls stopped coming in and both Anders and the driver turned in for a little sleep. At approx-imately 2 a.m. the loud bell, activated by the emergency room, jarred them awake. The caller's voice saying, "Apartment fire on Fourteenth and E Street," sent them scrambling toward the ambu-lance. Ezra, the driver, and Anders pulled on their coats as they left the warm room and climbed into the frigid ambulance. There was no heat in the garage. Ezra, who knew the city like the back of his hand having worked as an ambulance driver for sixteen years, knew that the apartments on Fourteenth and E Street were all five-story, cold-water, walk-up flats in a pretty bad part of town. There were no cars on the street, which was now solid ice, and the snowfall was almost horizontal as a stiff wind whipped through the sleeping city.

After a short ride they arrived at E Street where it was apparent that the whole five-story apartment building was ablaze, even though several fire trucks were pouring water through the broken windows. The firemen were running here and there as they tried to pull the heavy fire hoses into position. When the ambulance pulled up, a fireman ran up and shouted, "We need a doctor up there."

"Up where?" shouted Ezra.

"Up on the fifth floor."

Anders felt his heart pound, and in spite of the cold, began to sweat a little around his neck. What could a doctor do up in that horrible fire and smoke? He and Ezra climbed out of the ambulance with Anders carrying the large medical bag containing the various medicines and bandages used for most of the house calls. The minute they were out of the ambulance the icy wind cut through their coats and, even though they were near enough to the blazing inferno to feel the heat, they felt chilled to the bone.

The fireman, followed by Ezra and Anders, took off at a jog around a corner and into an alley. There were no streetlights but the fireman's flashlight provided a beacon, even though the smoke was fairly thick. All of a sudden the fireman stopped. This side of the building was almost free of flames and an enormous ladder reaching skyward from a ladder truck disappeared into the smoke. The fireman explained that this was the only way to get to the fifth floor and asked Anders if he wanted to go first or follow the fireman. The icy sweat on Anders' forehead and neck became more noticeable as he looked at the enormous ladder caked with a thin layer of ice, disappearing into the smoke in the dark.

"There must be some other way," stammered Anders.

"Nope," the fireman replied. "The stairwell in the building is in flames and there are no elevators."

"Is anybody up there alive?" Anders asked.

"Yep, but it's hard to tell who is alive and who is dead. We need your help. Here, I'll go first and carry your medical bag."

The fireman grabbed Anders' bag, climbed on the truck, and started up the ladder. Anders had experienced fear before, but it had never been anything like this. A small pain radiated through his chest as he started to climb the ladder. His thin gloves seemed totally inadequate to shield his hands from the icy rungs, and his eyes were burning from the smoke as he climbed rung-by-rung into the frightening unknown. The fireman above him had a flashlight hanging from his belt, which provided a feeble light and, after they had climbed a little over two stories, the fire broke through some windows below them and illuminated the whole ladder, now covered with ice leading to what seemed like an impossible goal.

One thing was certain—Anders would not look down, but step-by-step he continued up the ladder almost certain that he would be dead before this was over. All of a sudden he was looking into the arms of the fireman, who had climbed into a fifth-floor window and was pulling him in. The room was pitch-black except for the feeble flashlight darting back and forth through the smoke.

"They are over here," the fireman called as he pointed his light on a group of people partly covered by blankets. Some of them seemed to be moving; others were groaning and reaching out through the smoke.

The fireman said, "You have to tell me which ones to take out. I don't want to try to carry a corpse down that ladder."

Anders knelt in the dark, smoky room examining one person after another. No one answered his questions except for groans. It appeared they were not burnt but had been overcome by smoke and were barely conscious. Of the five people in the room three appeared to be dead, but two were clearly alive. Anders gave each a shot of morphine, and then one-by-one they were hoisted onto the shoulders of a fireman who disappeared out the window and down the ladder. Anders stood at the window and watched these brave men, one carrying a woman and the other a man down this icy ladder through the smoke and flames. As he watched he realized most of his fear had disappeared. Examining the patients and being part of this awful event had somehow increased his strength and confidence. After another check on the three who had certainly died, he gingerly climbed out the window and started down the ladder.

The spray from the fire hoses had reduced the flames but created more smoke, and it seemed the ice on the ladder was thicker. Carefully, step-by-step he backed down the five-story-high ladder and soon was greeting Ezra, who was waiting by the ladder truck. By now there were several more ambulances, fire hoses everywhere, police, and a few newspaper reporters.

Ezra smiled as he helped Anders off the fire truck and announced, "You had to be crazy to go up that ladder, but I have to admit that I am proud of you, you dummy."

They then loaded a badly burned patient into the ambulance and headed to the hospital. It was only when they entered the warm emergency room, which was crowded with burn patients, that Anders realized he was dripping wet and shivering. It was daylight when, after a hot shower and coffee and donuts, Ezra delivered Anders to the staff house where he said this was a night he would always remember.

Anders replied, "You are a master of the understatement."

— FOURTEEN —

THE DOG'S HEAD

In 1947, Anders' internship in Jersey City drew to a close and he received his summons from the Navy Department. It was time to pay back his obligation. He had agreed to serve two years of active duty for the privilege of being allowed to go to medical school rather than serving as a Second Lieutenant at Sea during the hostilities. His orders sent him to Anacostia Naval Station in Washington D.C. He drove down from Jersey City, found an apartment not far from the base and proceeded to acquire the requisite uniforms prior to reporting for duty. Luci exclaimed that he looked like a first-rate officer in his new Navy whites. She found an apartment not far from the naval base and they settled in with a new sense of financial security. Anders' salary was 600 dollars a month with another 100 dollars as a housing allowance.

He was assigned to the outpatient dispensary on the base, where he functioned as a general practitioner, dealing with day-to-day complaints of the sailors, aviators, and occasionally doing annual physicals on the officers who came to the base to get their exams. Most were from the Pentagon. He developed a friendship with many of the pilots, who regaled him with stories about flying from the deck of aircraft carriers during the war in the Pacific with the Japanese. They even introduced him to the flight simulator, where he learned some of the rudiments of flying in combat.

Life in Washington during the summer was stimulating. There were many sights to see including the Capitol, White House, museums, and concerts on the Potomac. Summer and fall passed quickly, and the coldest winter Washington had seen in years settled in. Anders' old 1937 Ford did not always start in the morning and it was becoming painfully apparent that his salary of 600 dollars a month, which had initially sounded great, was inadequate in a city where prices were anything but a bargain.

One morning after wading through two feet of snow to get to the bus because the old Ford wouldn't start, Anders found himself assigned to do an annual physical on Admiral Wainright, chief of the Naval Medical Corps. Anders mentioned the cold weather and low pay and how it was creating a considerable hardship.

The admiral remarked, "There's an opening at the naval hospital in Guantanamo Bay, Cuba. Would you like to go there? Living is cheap and I can guarantee there is no snow."

Anders jumped at the chance and Luci also agreed that it would be a great adventure, although she had begun to complain that being the wife of a naval doctor didn't seem like what she had envisioned when she agreed to marry Anders. Two weeks later Anders was on a naval transport plane for Gitmo with the plan that his wife would follow after he arranged for housing.

About 11 p.m. he disembarked at the Guantanamo Air Station and the balmy, tropical night with its air scented with night-blooming jasmines convinced him that this assignment in the Caribbean was going to be a great experience. During the next few days he lived at the BOQ (Bachelor Officers' Quarters), checked in with Captain Boomer, chief of the naval hospital, and was driven around the base by Commander Ducher, Assistant Medical

Officer, who helped him find housing, introduced him to the other six medical officers, and explained the routine.

The Guantanamo Naval Hospital was a one-story building with several wings and, like almost all facilities in Gitmo, had screens instead of windows. The little hospital was surrounded by beautiful palm trees, jasmines, and poinsettias, which provided a riot of color. A nurse explained that when the poinsettias bloom you know it's winter. That's the only sign.

About three weeks later Anders was assigned to a bungalow in the junior officer residential area, only about two blocks from the Officer's Club, which was the social center of the base, replete with bar, slot machines, a large pool, and a golf course. As he and his wife settled in they hired a nice Cuban woman as a house-keeper for thirty dollars a month and were convinced that they were in Paradise.

As a junior medical officer Anders took call every third night and every third weekend, and when he was on call he functioned as a family doctor, a surgeon, and an obstetrician. The second weekend of being on call, he was sitting around the hospital waiting for something to happen when in came the Shore Patrol with a dead dog. The dog had obviously been riddled with bullets. The Shore Patrol reported that this dog had viciously bitten a young child, the son of one of the chief petty officers on the base.

"The dog is probably rabid," the Shore Patrol claimed.

Anders remembered that the best way to diagnose rabies in a dog is to examine the brain. The only pathologist on the base was off duty, so they cut off the dog's head and to preserve it placed it in a freezing compartment of one of the large reefers in the hospital kitchen. The next morning Anders had an early hernia operation scheduled and for a time forgot all about the dog.

That morning a large contingent of admirals and other high-ranking officers from Washington were touring the hospital. They had come to evaluate Captain Boomer and his hospital as he was being considered for advancement to admiral. The captain was taking them on a tour of the hospital, which included the kitchen or galley. As the kitchen staff stood at attention while the brass paraded through, the chief in charge of the kitchen, who had been off duty the day before, threw open the reefer for inspection. The VIPs gasped as they viewed the dog's grizzly head sitting on the shelf staring out at them next to frozen steaks and other foodstuffs.

"What the hell is that?" shouted the captain.

"Looks like a dog," muttered the chief, who was as shocked as everyone else.

"Who put that in there?" bellowed the captain.

The chief looked at the other kitchen staff and one murmured, "Lieutenant JG Erickssen, sir."

The chief volunteered, "He's that new medical officer that came aboard about a month ago."

One of the admirals from Washington spoke up, "I hope the cleanliness of this hospital on the patient wards is better than in the galley."

No amount of explaining could convince the delegation from Washington that the standards of the rest of the hospital were much better. At 11 a.m. the assistant staff officer took the VIPs to the Officer's Club, and Captain Boomer went looking for Anders with blood in his eyes. When he found Anders, who had just finished surgery, he went into a rage. Anders' explanation about the dog's head fell on deaf ears.

"Do you know I was up for Admiral?" the captain screamed.

"No, sir," Anders muttered.

"You have ruined my future in the Navy Medical Corps. You will pay for this."

"Yes, sir," Anders responded as the captain turned on his heels and left the ward.

Anders decided not to tell the captain a week later when he found out that the dog did not have rabies.

The corpsmen who had overheard the outburst gathered around to console Anders, who now knew his future in the Naval Medical Corps looked bleak. Not that he had planned to sign up for conversion to a regular officer from the Naval Reserve after his obligatory duty was completed.

Several weeks went by without incident, but about one month later he was called into the captain's office. Anders didn't know if he would be court-martialed or what would happen. The captain was not in his office but his chief of staff, Commander Ducher, said, "The captain has assigned you an additional duty. You will be the base venereal disease control officer."

Anders asked, "What are the duties of the VD control officer?"

Ducher said, "The ships in the harbor allow their enlisted men to visit the bars in Caimanera when they are on shore leave, and the incidence of gonorrhea and syphilis has been rising. Your duty is to visit the brothels and find out a way to prevent sailors from getting infected."

"Sounds like a very difficult assignment, Commander."

"It's the worst assignment any medical officer could have, but you do have two corpsmen assigned to help you. This onerous duty is the old man's reward. You may not know, but he was passed over for Admiral and he considers it to be all your fault."

As Anders explained his plight to Luci that afternoon, hoping for a little sympathy, she retorted, "Serves you right for doing such a dumb thing. Just be careful dealing with those prostitutes in

Caimanera. I hear they are a pretty tough bunch. And don't come home with the CLAP."

"Well darling, if the captain orders me to go to Caimanera, I might as well enjoy it," Anders replied.

— FIFTEEN —

KING OF CAIMANERA

A nders' new assignment as Venereal Disease Control Officer was a blow to Luci. How could she explain to her religious family in Kentucky that her husband was going to be working with a bunch of prostitutes? The more she thought about it the angrier she got. How could Anders have done such a dumb thing? Would he become infected? What would the other Navy wives on the base think?

About ten miles across the bay from the Guantanamo Navy Base sat the Cuban city of Caimanera. Built on a mud flat, it had almost none of the charm of most Cuban towns and, although there were about 1,000 inhabitants, the main industry was the bars, of which there were about ten, built to attract American servicemen. Each bar was a substantial building with a brightly painted façade, with names like Sloppy Joe's, Havana Bar, Paradise Bar, and so on. Inside each building was a bar more than fifty feet long and a large dance floor surrounded by tables on one side and about ten or fifteen doors along the other. These doors led to the rooms or apartments where the "working girls" worked and lived. The rooms consisted of a double bed, a bathroom, a kitchenette, and some closet space.

The girls, about 150 in all, who occupied these rooms were the most important people in town and the richest. Several times a week liberty parties arrived by shore boat from the Navy ships in the harbor and deposited 700-800 sailors. This was where they got their R&R (rest and rehabilitation) while their ships were in the harbor. The attractions were girls, rum, and sex. The sailors sometimes danced, always drank, usually too much, and had sex. The income in Caimanera was almost totally generated by the bars and the girls. Each bar had a number one girl, the one who was the most in demand and who usually got the highest fees, although fees were individually negotiated on each contact. The owners of the bars collected from twenty-five to fifty percent of the girls' take and in exchange provided them with apartments and sometimes clothes or other favors.

In 1948 the Navy Department was beginning to get very concerned. The venereal disease rate among the Navy crews in the Caribbean was rising rapidly. They had recently provided the ships with a new antibiotic, penicillin, which was much more effective against syphilis than the previous mercurials and was also very effective against gonorrhea (clap). Anders decided that it was his duty to make the best of a bad situation and see if there was anything he could do to make it better. No matter what he did, Luci was not going to like it.

The word was out that controlling VD was of the highest priority—but how? Penicillin was a good treatment but it certainly didn't prevent acquiring the infection. These issues were explained to Anders after his assignment to VD Control by Commander Ducher. The next day he boarded a shore boat and made his first visit to Caimanera. The two corpsmen assigned to the VD detail had already alerted bar owners that the new VD officer wanted to meet the girls. In each bar the owners had the girls out in their Sunday best to meet the new doctor. Some of the girls, Anders thought, were quite pretty, but many had missing front teeth due to the custom of giving small children sugar cane to suck on. Anders thought to himself that the sailors would have to be pretty drunk to want to have sex with some of these women. All of the bar owners and some of the girls spoke and understood fairly good English. All were very friendly, and when informed that they were infecting American sailors they volunteered to do anything the doctor suggested to remedy the problem.

As Anders and the corpsmen were introduced to the girls it struck them that many had similar names and this would complicate their system of trying to pinpoint which girls were infecting the sailors. He explained to the number one girls and to the bar owners that when a sailor identified a girl as a possible contact the corpsman would come to the bar and examine the girls, take cultures and blood tests and, if they were infected, would treat them with penicillin for free.

"What if we refuse to be tested?" the girls countered.

Anders said, "I will recommend to the ships' commanders that Caimanera be off limits for liberty parties."

Although Anders had no idea if the ships' commanders would follow the suggestions of a lowly lieutenant JG medical officer, he thought it might get the attention of the Caimanera businesspeople.

Indeed, it did. If Anders could make this threat stick it would cut off the only source of income to the whole city. Everyone he talked to eagerly agreed to try the new plan.

In the next few weeks the corpsmen took pictures of each girl and gave each a number. Group pictures of all the girls in each bar were also taken. The pictures and the names and numbers of each girl were circulated to the medical officers on all the ships. When a sailor checked into the sick bay with a new case of clap or syphilis he was asked what girl he had sex with. Usually, the sailor couldn't remember her name but could usually pick her out from either the single or group photo. A call to the VD office on the base resulted in a corpsmen meeting with the girl the next day, and within a couple of days, if she tested positive, she was started on a course of penicillin and warned that she should remain unemployed for the next three weeks.

It turned out on the first go-round that thirty-two of the 150 girls had gonorrhea and four had syphilis. Within six months the incidence of VD in the fleet stationed in Guantanamo Bay and the sailors stationed on the base decreased from four percent to half a percent. A special commendation was awarded to the Guantanamo Naval Hospital by the Navy Department for this dramatic decrease, and Captain Boomer took full credit. Although he never congratulated Anders and the two corpsmen for their good work, his anger about not making full Admiral had somewhat abated.

Though Anders didn't receive any compliments from Captain Boomer for his efforts, the bar owners and the girls were appreciative. They realized that their source of income might have been jeopardized if the Navy had declared their town to be off limits to the liberty parties.

A gala congratulatory party was hosted by the bar owners and the prostitutes with Anders, his wife, and the two corpsmen as the guests of honor. The party was at Sloppy Joe's bar in Caimanera and a group of Anders' friends from the base and most of the prostitutes of Caimanera attended. Luci at first refused to go but she was urged to attend by so many of the Navy wives that she finally relented. Anders was crowned King of Caimanera and danced with many of the girls who believed their livelihood had been salvaged by the VD team and the Navy supplies of penicillin. Anders' status as King of Caimanera turned out to be somewhat of a celebrity issue on the base and the other officers and corpsmen called him King Kay, either as a term of endearment or as a slightly derogatory joke.

The remainder of Anders' stay at Gitmo resulted in his gaining a good deal of experience in orthopedics, during his second assignment in the hospital, even though he had never had any formal training in this specialty. Also, during his off hours he played a good deal of golf and, under the tutelage of Commander Ducher, he felt he had become fairly proficient.

As the end of his two years of obligated Navy duty became imminent, the disagreements with Luci became more serious. Should they separate when he returned to Jersey City for his medical residency? They certainly couldn't live on his meager salary, even if they could find a way to get along.

SIXTEEN

THE RETURN TO JERSEY CITY

After his discharge from the Navy Anders returned to Jersey City for his medical residency. His salary was to be only 100 dollars a month plus food and lodging. There was no way with this limited income that he could support his growing family, which now included his wife and two children. It was decided that Luci and the kids would go to Auburn and live with Anders' parents for the year. Even though it was somewhat of a hardship for them, Anders' parents agreed. They had heard about some of Anders' disagreements with Luci and weren't looking forward to spending a year with her and having to listen to her complaints.

The work schedule at Jersey City Medical Center for a first-year resident required that the resident take call every other night, and although it was arduous it turned out to be a seminal part of Anders' training. There were eight residents in the internal medicine program, and the guiding force was the chief resident, Carroll Levey. Dr. Levey was a black physician who, at the time, seemed to be the smartest and best-informed doctor Anders had ever met. Early on, Dr. Levey realized that Anders was ambitious and energetic and, therefore, piled on the workload and extra assignments. He asked Anders to make presentations at conferences and ward rounds and assigned him to a research project evaluating a new mercurial diuretic, Thiomerin, which led to Anders' first published paper.

Because Levey pushed him relentlessly, Anders became convinced that he was a favorite of the boss, which drove him to prove himself, a trait that endured throughout his career in medicine. A special opportunity was afforded Anders due to his special relationship with Dr. Levey.

One of the special privileges Dr. Levey orchestrated was in the field of cardiology. He suggested that Anders start learning how to take an electrocardiogram. In 1946, the manipulation and calibration of a string galvanometer was a coveted skill in medical circles and Marie Sinkowski was not about to share it with many others. She had been trained at the Mass General Hospital in Boston several years before and was the only person in the Jersey City Medical Center who knew how to operate the device.

Although the string galvanometer, a machine that had been invented by Dutch engineer Einthoven in 1860, was beginning to be recognized as an important tool in the diagnosis of cardiac arrhythmias, its complexity had limited its use. The process—which consisted of warming up the coils and carefully balancing the electrical currents prior to attaching it to the patient with special electrodes after abrading the skin with sandpaper and applying a jelly mixed with salt—usually took more than half an hour. The light focused on the string and cast a shadow that recorded onto a photographic film a very low-level current generated by the heart. The device was mounted on a cart but weighed over 200 pounds and was not very portable. The electrical record had been shown by Einthoven and others to be the best way to study the heart's rhythm, which had a good deal of influence on heart function.

Marie Sinkowski agreed to teach Anders how to make these recordings only after he had pleaded, negotiated, and cajoled her for several months. Anders had also emphasized that Dr. Levey wanted him to learn to make these tracings. Although, in Anders' eyes, Marie was not much to look at, being twenty years older than him, he showered her with compliments, brought her sweet rolls and donuts, and finally convinced her that he was worthy of this special treatment. He was really excited to be initiated into an elite group of individuals who would be learning new things about the heart.

The instruction lasted several hours off and on for about ten sessions before Marie was confident that her new technician would make a high-quality recording that would not damage her valuable equipment. As Anders suspected, this special skill would set him apart among the residents and attending staff, as one who had special knowledge about the heart, although in 1949 the specialty of cardiology was not recognized as such. The specialty of internal medicine, the area Anders was pointing toward, was expected to know all there was to know about the heart.

During these early weeks of indoctrination into the mysteries of the string galvanometer he often wondered if his childhood diagnosis of rheumatic heart disease had been correct or if a functional murmur had been misdiagnosed by Dr. Russell, the family physician.

As the year of his residency drew to a close he yearned to be with his family, even though his married life in Guantanamo had been stormy, to say the least. He needed to find a residency with more income. One of the attending internists told Anders of a residency in Long Beach, California, supervised by Dr. Fred Kellogg, one of his classmates at Harvard. The internist told Anders, "With your interest in electrocardiography, you couldn't go wrong with Fred Kellogg. He knows more about electrocardiography than almost anyone. Besides, he will pay you a living wage." A few weeks later, after a several phone calls from Dr. Kanjame in Jersey

City to Fred Kellogg, Anders was offered a residency at Seaside Hospital in Long Beach. The salary was 150 dollars a month and an apartment. Anders told his wife that they would be a family again, and it was well received. He believed that this time he could make his marriage work.

And so Anders planned to head home to California at the end of the year. How to get there at the lowest cost? A Greyhound bus seemed like the best bet, but he heard a radio broadcast describing a transcontinental commercial flight from Newark, New Jersey, to Oakland, California, for only 100 dollars. The airline was called The Flying Irishman. Anders called and made the reservation and early one morning found himself on a converted U.S. Air Force cargo plane with bucket seats, headed for California.

The fuselage had a few holes here and there, and the noise was deafening. He was surely glad his old Navy raincoat had a liner because even in July it was pretty cold at 10,000 feet. The radio advertisement had implied that this was a nonstop flight. The Flying Irishman turned out to have many stops, the first of which was Baltimore, the next Des Moines, the third Dallas, and so forth. When night fell it got a lot colder and at about midnight they stopped in Denver to refuel. The passengers were given snacks, which probably had been K rations from the war surplus store, and were warned that the next leg would be over the Rocky Mountains and would be up to 14,000 feet. Anders knew that most of the high peaks in the Rockies were about 12,000 feet and wondered whether a 2,000-foot clearance was enough. The fellow functioning as a flight attendant opined that because they had no oxygen they didn't feel safe going any higher.

They took off for the West at about 2 a.m. and at about the time of takeoff Anders began to get a burning pain in his right lower abdomen. He also became a little nauseated. As they gained altitude the nausea got worse and soon he was vomiting into a plastic bag provided for those with air sickness. The flight attendant assured Anders that on the west side of the Rockies the air would be smoother and they would descend to 10,000 feet, where he would feel better. Anders was miserable but certain that the pain in his right side was not air sickness. He suspected he had acute appendicitis. During the next hours the pain waxed and waned, as did his nausea. "I just hope my appendix doesn't rupture," he murmured to himself. Finally they touched down at Oakland Airport. It was midmorning of the trip's second day.

Commander Ducher, Anders' friend from Guantanamo, who had been reassigned to the Oakland Naval Hospital, had agreed to meet the flight. As Anders stumbled off the plane and saw his friend, he was very relieved. "Dutch, get me to a surgeon. I need my appendix out." Within a short time Dutch delivered Anders to the surgical ward at the Oakland Naval Hospital, and about two hours later Anders was in the operating room having his appendix removed. Spinal anesthesia made it possible for Anders to discuss his problem with the surgeon and with Dutch during the procedure.

It was with great relief that his diagnosis was confirmed to be correct and that the appendix had not ruptured. After three days in the hospital Dutch delivered Anders to Auburn, where, looking slightly pale, he was reunited with his family after one full year.

SEVENTEEN

IOWA BY THE SEA

After a few days Anders and Luci bought the cheapest six-cylinder Ford coupe on the market with their last 900 dollars, loaded the kids in back on a mattress, and headed for Long Beach. Although Anders had grown up in California he had never been to Long Beach. When they arrived, the family was delighted with the "little city by the sea" but when they got to Seaside Hospital, which had only three stories and four wings and 300 beds, they were a little disappointed. Compared to the twelve-story tower at Jersey City Medical Center with 1,200 beds, it looked pretty Podunk.

Shortly after they arrived in the lobby, however, they were greeted by pathologist Joe Tuta and Elleston Farrell, the chief of medicine. After a hearty meal in the hospital cafeteria they met Calvin Lauer, chief of surgery. He was a polished, impressive man about six feet three inches with white hair and a warm, friendly face. "You've never been to Long Beach before? Why don't you take my car, cruise around, and see if you like it? We all think it's one of the best little cities in the West." He led them to the parking lot, where they were deposited into the longest white Cadillac convertible they had ever seen. It was a beautiful, balmy, sunny day and as they drove down Ocean Boulevard, gazing out at the blue Pacific and five-mile-long beach, they all agreed that this place was about as good as Guantanamo.

Although the apartment they had been assigned to was a little cramped, it was big enough and was about half a block from the hospital. In the days that followed, Anders met and became acquainted with the only other medical resident—Don Cruise—the interns, and Fred Kellogg, who had been so highly praised in Jersey City.

The year in Long Beach provided Anders an opportunity to develop some leadership skills, as he was appointed chief resident and spent a good deal of time teaching the interns. He also spent time with Joe Tuta in the pathology department. He became convinced that if he were going to be a top-flight internist he should also be an expert in pathology. Joe Tuta showed him the way, and Fred Kellogg sharpened his knowledge of electrocardiography.

Patients with heart attacks, which were many, were kept in the hospital for three weeks at bed rest and were all given Dicumeral. The term was *coronary thrombosis* and the anticoagulant was designed to dissolve the thrombus in the coronary arteries. About this time, Hans Selye, from Montreal, was explaining about the alarm reaction and its effect on the body as a whole. Anders had heard him lecture in Los Angeles and describe the eosinopenia that occurred during the time of maximum stress. Anders surmised that the degree of eosinopenia might help determine the severity of the myocardial infarction (heart attack). Thereafter, each day when blood was drawn to measure the prothombin time in the infarct patients, Anders counted the eosinophils. Sure enough, the number of eosinophils decreased dramatically. Here was a blood test, the first one, that would measure the severity of an acute myocardial infarction because the larger the area of injury to the heart, the more the stress. So Anders published his second paper. Coming up with a new idea was exhilarating. It was and always would be.

Anders' idea was presented to Dr. George Griffith, who by this time was being recognized as "Mr. Cardiology" in Los Angeles. After meeting with Anders, Griffith suggested he spend his third year in the new USC program just being initiated. For the first time in Los Angeles the specialty of cardiology was being introduced. Unfortunately, Anders had already signed a contract with San Francisco County Hospital to spend a year in pathology. Much to his disappointment Anders was unable to accept the very special opportunity at USC. His friends at Seaside said, "Just break your contract in San Francisco." Anders could not bring himself to break a contract he had signed in good faith.

– EIGHTEEN –

SAN FRANCISCO COUNTY HOSPITAL

The year at Seaside seemed to literally fly by. It appeared that another year in clinical medicine would require less expertise than a thorough knowledge of the pathology of diseases. Anders' interactions with Joe Tuta, the pathologist at Seaside, had honed his appetite for a year in the laboratory. Joe seemed to Anders to be very bright and had a homespun humor that tickled Anders. One day as Anders was watching Joe do an autopsy, as Joe resected the breast bone he looked at Anders and remarked with a sly grin, "If you are ever doing an autopsy and get this far and resect the sternum and see that the heart is still beating, cut it out in a hurry. That way you won't have to answer any tough questions."

As noted, on Joe's advice Anders had applied for and been accepted to a straight pathology residency at San Francisco County Hospital in the University of California service. Shortly after, the offer from George Griffith had to be rejected, even though Anders suspected that he would often wonder if he had made a wise choice. In preparation for his new residency, Anders prepared about twenty case histories of unusual patients he had seen at Seaside who had microscopic slides of either surgical or autopsy specimens.

These cases went with him partly to check on Dr. Tuta's diagnosis but also to show the pathologists at UC and his new chief, Jessie Carr, that the new resident knew a little something before starting the program.

Upon arriving in San Francisco Anders found an apartment in a large complex, Park Merced, where a number of other medical residents lived. The complex had a wide landscaped park and was adjacent to Lake Merced, which added to the ambiance. The only problem was that it was foggy a good deal of the time. However, when Anders drove across town to the county hospital, he always seemed to break out into the sunshine.

The pathology program at San Francisco County was made to order for Anders. Not only was there a large volume of surgical specimens to study, but also many autopsies. He soon found that the other pathology residents didn't like to do autopsies, so he volunteered to do theirs as well as his own. Searching for the cause of death was often a real challenge, which intrigued Anders and stimulated him to immerse himself in textbooks and research articles pertaining to these cases. It was 1951, and it was becoming apparent that cancer of the lung was almost never seen in a non-smoker. One of Anders' first presentations to the UC Grand Rounds was to demonstrate this relationship, which generated a great deal of discussion and special praise from his chief, Jessie Carr.

The other autopsy patients that intrigued Anders were those brought in from the coroner's office with sudden death. As Anders carefully dissected out the coronary arteries, the severity of the coronary narrowing, which often involved almost the whole length of the artery, was a real eye-opener. Most of the medical books had suggested that a few high-grade local obstructions were the most common findings. Anders found single localized obstruction to be extremely rare, which suggested that our understanding of the cause of this disease was still rudimentary—a fact that would linger in Anders' mind long after bypass surgery and methods to dissolve the clots for acute myocardial infarction were instituted.

One day at lunch one of the medical residents reminded Anders, "Don't miss Grand Rounds tomorrow. A very colorful attorney will speak. His name is Melvin Belli." Anders, up to this time, did not know any attorneys and had not given them or the laws relating to medicine much thought. Malpractice cases were practically unheard of. The next morning, the auditorium was almost full for what turned out to be a rude awakening for most of the residents and medical faculty.

Belli, who was quite grandiose in his manner and who dressed in a very stylish, expensive suit with large gold cufflinks, reiterated this sermon. The theme was "Don't make a contract with your patients." Anders had always thought that a good doctor tried to convince his patients how concerned he was about the patient and, in effect, made an implied contract to do his best for him. Belli told this story. A man, working for a low wage, was thirty-five years old and had already four children. He was having a hard time making ends meet and had heard about a vasectomy as a way to keep from having any more children. He went to a urologist for help in limiting his family. The urologist said, "After I've done a vasectomy, you won't have any more children. Guaranteed!" In other words, he made an implied contract. About six months later the man returned to the urologist in a very bad mood. He said, "Doc, you lied to me. My wife is pregnant." The urologist responded, "Well, let's get a sperm sample." When the doctor found that his patient had no sperm, and explained that he was not the father of the pregnancy, the patient charged out of the office in a rage.

"About two months later," Belli boasted, "he came to see me on the advice of a friend. I explained to him that it didn't matter if his wife's pregnancy was by someone else. The doctor had contracted with him not to have any more children. We won a malpractice suit based on a breach of contract. We got him two hundred thousand dollars" (a ton of money in 1951). Anders and most of the other doctors were outraged. When they castigated Belli during the question-and-answer period he just laughed, "This is the way the law was interpreted. Just keep it in mind. Don't make contracts." From that day on Anders understood what constituted legal ethics. There is no morality—just what you can get away with in the courts. It was several years later before Anders learned that Belli, who became a celebrity in San Francisco, was not representative of the legal profession.

As the year passed Anders began looking for a place to practice. He had an offer from Drs. Elleston Farrell and Fred Clark in Long Beach. Both of these men were physicians whom he admired intensely, but Luci was agitating to get Anders to stay in Northern California. Offers from Kaiser in San Francisco, internists in Santa Rosa and Modesto, just didn't seem right. So, in July 1952 the family packed up and returned to Long Beach. Anders opted to join Farrell and Clark for a salary of 700 dollars a month with a partnership available after two years. He was never sorry.

NINETEEN

AFTERLOAD REDUCTION

L ong Beach and Seaside Hospital in 1952 were ideal for Anders. Very soon he was busy seeing patients, teaching the interns and residents at Seaside, and making house calls for Drs. Farrell and Clark. An office call cost the patient four dollars, while a house call cost six dollars. Many patients would rather pay the extra two dollars to have the doctor come to their home. Dr. Farrell particularly was happy to pass on his house calls to Anders, who was happy to see patients anytime anywhere.

UCLA Medical School had just set up a teaching service at Harbor Hospital in Torrance, California, and Long Beach internists were volunteering to serve as teachers. By doing so they were awarded a clinical appointment as assistant professors (without pay, of course). Anders volunteered and soon became very involved in the program. So involved, in fact, that a few years later he was elected chief of staff at Harbor Hospital.

It was Thursday morning and Anders was presenting to the UCLA Grand Rounds at Harbor Hospital. His excitement was engendered by the results he would report on his new treatment for pulmonary edema. It promised to be a major breakthrough in treating this severe manifestation of congestive heart failure.

Because after starting practice in Long Beach he had volunteered to be on call for Seaside Hospital emergency room, he frequently was called to see patients admitted with severe pulmonary edema. This rather sudden manifestation of heart failure resulted in severe shortness of breath, marked anxiety, and a feeling in patients that they would suffocate. An examination revealed that their lungs were full of fluid. The standard treatment consisted of placing the patient in an oxygen tent, putting tourniquets on his or her arms and legs to reduce the blood returning to the heart, and injecting morphine to treat the extreme anxiety. If the patient got better or failed to do so it would take three or four hours. Anders found that almost all of these patients had severe high blood pressure, and he reasoned that an increase in blood pressure would increase cardiac work and certainly couldn't be good for a failing heart.

One evening, as Anders was watching a seventy-four-year-old woman with severe high blood pressure struggle for her breath, he decided to reduce her blood pressure. A new medicine, hexamathonium, had just been released and when injected intravenously would cause a rapid and dramatic drop in blood pressure. He injected five milligrams of hexamathonium intravenously into this woman and in two or three minutes her systolic blood pressure dropped from 230 to 120 millimeters of mercury. He was about to elevate her legs to prevent any further drop when she responded, "Doctor, I feel so much better. I'm breathing easier already."

This marked improvement within five minutes of the blood pressure drop was something Anders had never seen before. Within twenty minutes the patient was breathing almost normally, the breath sounds revealing much less congestion, the cyanosis gone from her lips, and instead of her previous look of panic she was smiling. Anders was elated.

He soon made a deal with Bill Olsen, a medical resident, and they took turns covering the emergency room at Seaside every other night for the next six months. Every patient with acute pulmonary edema got better when his or her blood pressure was reduced. Anders and Bill could hardly wait to spread the good news. Anders arranged with Dr. Lawrence, the chief of medicine at UCLA, to present his findings at a hospital Grand Rounds. There were over seventy-five doctors in attendance. When Anders finished describing his new treatment he was expecting a thundering applause. But, no applause! Anders was stunned. As Anders stood there, Dr. Lawrence stood up and remarked, "If anyone in this hospital uses this treatment, he will be fired on the spot!"

A few months later, when Anders presented the same talk at the Scientific Session of the American Heart Association in New Orleans, his first national meeting, the reception was almost as chilling as it had been at UCLA, even though the chairman of the meeting, Dr. Sarnoff, who had just been appointed chief of the new cardiology section at the National Institute of Health, congratulated Anders and advised him, "Keep working on this. It sounds like a good idea." It was only after, nearly ten years later, Drs. Swan and Ganz demonstrated that reducing the blood pressure would increase the cardiac output, that Anders' treatment became an accepted practice. It was labeled "after-load reduction." No one, however, gave Anders any credit for being the first to conceive of the idea, proving that sometimes a good idea is hard to accept if someone else thinks of it first.

In 1953, one year after Anders had arrived in Long Beach, a new doctor appeared at Seaside—Julian Knutson. Knutson immediately took to Anders, as they were both Norwegian. He had just finished a cardiology fellowship at Mayo Clinic, one of the few in the country at the time teaching heart catheterizations. Soon the UCLA medical group at Harbor was proposing that Julian open up a catheterization laboratory at their hospital. It would be the second one in the Los Angeles basin, the first being at L.A. County, which had been started about three years before. Because Knutson and Anders hit it off famously, Julian said that if he started a lab he wanted Anders to help him.

Anders was excited. He had read about this new procedure, and the chance to be involved was a unique opportunity. So, once a week Julian and Anders labored under a primitive fluoroscope after wearing dark glasses for fifteen minutes, passing catheters into the right atrium, right ventricle, and pulmonary artery to take blood samples and oxygen saturations. Soon, Julian and Anders revisited Mayo Clinic to get advice on where to obtain an oximeter that could also be used to calculate cardiac output (the pumping action of the heart). Anders' new activity took quite a bit of extra time away from his practice, which reduced his income, much to his wife's disgust. Things were going well in his professional life but his marriage was turning out to be a catastrophe. Luci resented all the time Anders was spending at Harbor Hospital and not earning any money, and had other complaints as well. The catheterization lab added new dimensions to Anders' understanding of cardiac physiology, however, and he was deeply involved.

– TWENTY –

LILY ENG

An intriguing Chinese lady, Lily Eng, sought Anders' help because her exercise tolerance was decreasing. She had a Caucasian husband and operated a very popular Chinese restaurant in Long Beach, where she had become something of a celebrity. Anders immediately recognized that she had mitral stenosis and might benefit from a new valve surgery. The year before, Dr. Mickey Beland, who had finished a cardiac surgical residency at Harbor Hospital, was induced to set up practice in Long Beach by Anders, who had been impressed by his performance during his training. Now it was time to resume mitral valve surgery at Seaside, pioneered by Dr. Charles Bailey six years before.

Late in 1951, while Anders was a medical resident at Seaside, a special event in the operating room captivated his attention. Although Theodor Billroth, the super-surgeon from Vienna, who had pioneered many operations on the GI tract and headed the most prestigious surgical program in Europe, had admonished all surgeons in about 1910 to never try to operate on the heart, in 1948 Bailey, from Philadelphia, had figured out a way to insert his finger into the left atrium (upper chamber) of the beating heart and open a narrowed mitral valve that had been damaged by rheumatic fever.

He had come to Long Beach and operated on two patients with mitral stenosis at Seaside Hospital and had left an indelible imprint on Anders. Six years later Anders was doing catheterizations on patients with mitral stenosis, and several large centers across the U.S. were following Charles Bailey's lead. Charles Lindbergh, probably the most famous celebrity in the world at the time, had spent time in New York in 1938 with Alexis Correl, the famous French experimental surgeon, trying to invent a heart-lung machine because his sister had mitral stenosis. His efforts failed, partly because he did not yet know how to prevent blood clotting. Heparin had yet to be discovered.

Because of Anders' growing reputation for being involved in cardiology, patients were beginning to seek him out. Very few internists referred patients to him because the internists all believed that they knew enough about heart disease to make their own decisions; however, family practitioners were beginning to send some referrals.

Lily agreed to the surgery, and with Anders hovering over him Dr. Beland opened Lily's chest and inserted his finger into her atrium. Dr. Beland looked at Anders with alarm. "There's a large clot in the atrial cavity. I believe it is not attached to anything. If it goes through the heart and into her circulation, she will have a massive stroke."

Here they were, embarking for the first time on this dangerous operation, facing a catastrophe in a patient to whom they both become very attached. With his index finger still in Lily's atrial cavity, Dr. Beland said to his surgical assistant, "Hand me a number two suture on a curved needle. I think I can hold the clot against the wall with my index finger and sew it to the atrial wall from the outside so it will re-anchor and not form an embolus." As he proceeded to attempt to perform what Anders thought was a brilliant idea, he suddenly reported, "It's gone."

Anders' and Mickey Beland's hearts sank. Where would it end up? Over the next three or four minutes, with both men's hearts pounding, Anders kept examining Lily's pupils. "No change. Maybe it missed her head." He then burrowed under the drapes to feel the pulses in her legs. "Hooray, it's in her leg. She has no pulse in the left foot." After Mickey finished the commisurotomy (opening the valve), and after closing the chest he turned to her groin. Eventually the femoral artery was opened, the embolus removed, and normal flow restored to the leg. Late that afternoon when Lily was out of the O.R. and waking up in the recovery room, Anders and Dr. Beland explained the process to her husband and later, as they sat in the locker room, they congratulated themselves on their good fortune as well as that of Lily Eng, who was lucky to have had the clot go to her leg and not to her head.

One month later Lily and her husband put on a gala banquet at the restaurant for Mickey Beland and Anders, to celebrate what might have been a terrible event that turned out to be the kickoff to many years of very successful collaboration.

TWENTY-ONE

MAYO CLINIC

J ulian Knutson, who grew up in Wadina, Minnesota, was convinced that Mayo Clinic was the center of technical know-how in cardiology. His chief there, Earl Woods, admittedly was one of the very innovative cardiologists in the U.S. At that time Mayo Clinic was one of only four or five cardiology training programs in the country. About the time Julian had started his training, Mayo Clinic's new ultra centrifuge was installed. This enormous device consisted of a small seat instrumented so that the blood pressure, with a brachial artery needle and pulmonary pressure with an indwelling catheter inserted through the brachial vein along with respiratory gas, could be analyzed while the subject was rotated at the end of a thirty-foot beam. Thus, G forces could be produced that would simulate those experienced while flying the newer fighter planes and dive bombers.

This laboratory, funded by the new U.S. Air Force, helped determine how our aviators would tolerate the maneuvers necessary during combat. Earl Woods' research was facilitated by the fact that those in the cardiology training program served as subjects on the centrifuge. Julian said he dreaded the times when it was his turn to be the subject. It was bad enough having needles inserted into his radial artery and catheters in his heart, but during the test they would spin the centrifuge at increasing speeds until he would almost pass out—a miserable experience. In the early days when cardiology was in its infancy it was common for the doctors, who were trainees, to also be experimental subjects. It was the price you paid to be part of an exciting new area of knowledge.

Julian had enormous respect for Earl Woods, as did everyone else in the country. Julian, therefore, proposed that he and Anders would visit his old chief to get his advice on the type of instrumentation they should acquire for their catheterization laboratory in the new hospital now under construction. Upon their arrival in Rochester, Minnesota, after an extensive discussion, Dr. Woods advised them that there was no commercially available system that was ideal. He then drew up an outline of the specifications they should require if they could find an *engineer* to build their cath lab physiological recorder. He did suggest that the purchase of a Water's oximeter, made there in Rochester, would be helpful, as it would not only allow them to measure the oxygen content of the blood but also calculate cardiac output.

It was a stimulating experience for Anders to meet Dr. Woods and be able to quiz him on a number of ideas being generated as he went through the Mayo lab and talked to the other cardiologists working there. After two days in the catheterization laboratory Julian announced that it was time to leave Mayo Clinic and head north to his hometown, Wadina. A duck hunting trip with Julian's two brothers was being planned. It was late October and although the days were sunny, the temperature in Wadina at night was dipping below freezing.

After a big family dinner everyone slept for a few hours and then got up at 3 a.m., loaded into the family truck, and headed north to Leach Lake, one of the numerous lakes near the Canadian border. Upon arrival Anders was bundled into an oversized waterproof hunting outfit and supplied with a twelve-gauge double-barreled shotgun. It was still dark but the frigid night sky was just beginning to turn gray when they all climbed into a small outboard motorboat at a small landing, specifically designed for duck hunters. As Anders' teeth chattered from the cold, he was also apprehensive that there were only about six or eight inches of freeboard separating the occupants of the boat from the black, icy water.

As they chugged out into the lake, towing a second boat full of decoys, Anders complained that he was so cold he doubted he would be able to aim a shotgun. The response was to hand him a whiskey bottle saying, "This will warm your cockles." They also kidded him about the fact that Norwegians who had moved from Minnesota to California had gone soft. They laughed, "We hear you even have warm snow in California." As they motored out into the lake, dawn began to illuminate the size of the body of water they were in. To Anders, the opposite shore seemed like it was thirty miles away. After about half an hour they reached a shallow area where numerous clumps of reeds provided some protection from the frigid wind that ripped the water into little whitecaps. There they dispersed the decoys over an area of about fifty yards and settled down to wait for the birds and enjoy another "warmer-upper."

Soon the birds began to appear, heralded by their honking calls. Julian got out his duck caller, and within a few minutes flocks of ducks were heading for the decoys, where they were met with rapid fire from four shotguns. It sounded like a war. After each flock was fired upon the group of hunters started up the outboard motor and picked the ducks up out of the water. Within a short time they had four limits and headed back to the landing. Anders was glad to get into the warm truck cab and began to feel pretty good by the time they arrived back in Wadina for a hearty, mid-morning breakfast. This seemed like a perfect ending to a successful sporting event, but Anders felt that duck hunting in Minnesota was not for him.

That afternoon, on their way south to the Minneapolis airport, Anders admitted to Julian that the trip to Mayo Clinic was fantastic but he was very glad that duck hunting was behind him. He said he had skied in some very cold days but didn't remember a time when he had experienced the type of cold featured on a duck hunting trip in Minnesota. Julian laughed, "Norwegians are supposed to be tough. If you had complained of the cold to my brothers they would have accused you of being a Swede. That's as bad as it gets."

After they arrived home a few days later, the ultimate disappointment occurred when they ate the ducks. The meat was so full of buckshot that it was a challenge to chew it without losing a few teeth.

TWENTY-TWO

THE NEW HOSPITAL
AND A TRIP TO CLEVELAND

In 1960, Seaside Hospital moved to a new 400-bed facility and was renamed Long Beach Memorial Hospital. They agreed to provide a two-room laboratory for the budding cardiologists, Knutson and Erickssen. The small space was next to the X-ray department, where they planned to do their heart catheterizations in a room designed for GI X-rays. The chief of radiology, Hugh Pritchard, rationalized that heart catheterizations were of little value and would soon disappear, so he didn't mind sharing his space with the "Swedes," as he called them—the term was not one of endearment. Julian and Anders were fully aware that the internists at Seaside resented that some of their group were claiming to have special skills and knowledge related to heart disease, which had been validated by their developing a catheterization laboratory at Harbor Hospital under the auspices of UCLA School of Medicine. So, they reasoned, what should we call our new space? They came up with "Clinical Physiology," which would not sound too presumptuous.

In this area they set up a treadmill, a phonocardiogram, and a spirometer to do simple pulmonary function tests. As advised by Earl Woods from Mayo, they had an engineer, Chet Smith, build a physiological recorder with two pressure channels, an ECG channel, and an electroencephalogram. This could be taken to the cath lab in the X-ray department or into the operating room to monitor cardiac surgery. A door opened from their laboratory into the back end of the X-ray department, so they could take their patients in for heart catheterizations. The patients consisted mostly of children and young people with congenital heart disease as well as older patients with rheumatic valvular disease.

After a time, Anders spent a few weeks in the National Institute of Health Cardiac Center in Bethesda, Maryland, learning to do transeptal punctures, a procedure where a long needle was passed from the groin up the veins to puncture the atrial septum, the wall between the heart's two upper chambers. This gave direct access to the left side of the heart and improved the diagnosis of valvular disease. When Anders returned from Bethesda, much to his dismay Julian announced, "Anders, I have decided I will not do any more heart catheterizations. I just don't have the stomach for it." In spite of Anders' vigorous objections, Julian abdicated the very procedure he had taught Anders to do, leaving Anders as the only physician in the hospital doing heart catheterizations. It was at this time that Harbor/UCLA retained a cardiologist from Chicago, Steve Liu, to take over the procedures, relieving Julian and Anders of their volunteer work at Harbor.

A year before, a new hospital in Long Beach had opened. At an American College of Cardiology meeting, Anders had heard a presentation given by Mason Sones from Cleveland. In the next two or three years Sones presented angiograms of coronary arteries at each annual meeting, demonstrating that for the first time it was possible to get a clear picture of what was going on in the arteries that constituted the gas line to the heart.

In 1962, Hugh Pritchard, the chief of radiology, purchased a new X-ray system with image amplifiers and a rapid camera for GI X-rays. Anders knew this system could also be used to image the coronary arteries, so he called Dr. Sones in Cleveland and made an appointment to spend two weeks there to learn to do coronary angiograms. His first day in Cleveland was exciting. Sones, who was very friendly, had Anders scrub up with him and proceeded to demonstrate his technique of localizing and cutting down on the brachial artery, just above the elbow, under local anesthetic. Once the artery was exposed and opened and a catheter was inserted, he turned to Anders and said, "How about a smoke?" Anders was abashed. The scrub nurse lit a cigarette and handed it to Dr. Sones, who proceeded to puff on the noxious weed while, under fluoroscopic vision, maneuvering the catheter up the artery into the chest and into the coronary artery. Anders declined the offer to follow suit with a cigarette.

As they dimmed the lights so that they could see the catheter better on the X-ray screen, the bright cigarette ash glowed and the smoke curled around Dr. Sones' head. Within a few days, under Dr. Sones' tutelage, Anders was beginning to get the knack of maneuvering the catheter into the ostium "opening" of the coronary arteries. With the camera running and recording moving pictures while he injected dye, the arteries lit up in great detail. Anders learned to pass the catheter across the aortic valve so they could inject dye into the cavity of the heart and evaluate visually how well the heart was pumping and determine if abnormalities in the valves were present.

During his stay there he also met a charming Argentinean surgeon, who was in and out of Sones' laboratory. Dr. Favolaro was doing experimental surgery in the animal lab and would soon become famous for introducing bypass surgery. By the end of two weeks, Anders was confident he had learned to do something that would open up a whole new avenue of investigation and treatments for coronary artery disease, the prevalence of which was increasing rapidly, partly due to the generalized use of cigarettes. Anders recognized that those who could do this test really deserved to be called cardiologists. He went home to Long Beach with a package of new Sones' catheters and changed the name of his laboratory from Clinical Physiology to the department of Cardiology. Now, patients who had evidence of coronary artery disease on the treadmill could have a definitive diagnostic test. This was soon to be followed by the direct surgical attack on the coronary arteries using the procedure Favolaro would demonstrate.

Before long, Anders attracted a great deal of attention with his coronary angiograms, and within a few months a new cardiac surgeon, William Bloomer, transferred his activities from the UCLA program at Harbor Hospital to Memorial. His research helped in the introduction of the "Vineburg Operation" in Long Beach, based on the demonstration by Anders of the obstruction in the coronary arteries.

The Vineburg procedure, introduced by a Canadian surgeon, consisted of inserting a small artery from the chest wall into the heart muscle, where collaterals (connections) formed with the small arteries leading to the heart muscle. For a time no one believed the operation did any good until Mason Sones injected dye into the internal mammary artery and demonstrated that it did indeed connect with coronary arteries. Anders did exercise tests before and after the surgery, demonstrating objectively that patients with Vineburg procedures were indeed improved. It was an exciting time and soon a training program was established where graduates from the internal medicine residency were signing on to learn to be cardiologists.

The new Memorial Hospital was beginning to be recognized as an outstanding cardiology center, and Anders' reputation as its chief cardiologist continued to grow. Sometimes Anders would wonder at the rapid pace of the specialty and would acknowledge how fortunate he had been to get in on the ground floor, as it were, and to be in an environment that would allow him to pursue new ideas.

TWENTY-THREE

THE TREADMILL

In 1965, the hospital administration decided it was time to computerize some of its bookkeeping. They purchased a mainframe CDC computer with an input scanner that would read printed forms. The assistant hospital administrator, Ray Lake, decided he needed to learn more about computers and suggested to Anders that they both attend a six-month course being offered by IBM in Los Angeles. For six months they drove to Los Angeles two nights a week. As Anders learned about how computers work and how to program in FORTRAN, the computer language commonly used in scientific programs, he realized how much power this system could give him in cardiology if used properly.

When they were finished with their introductory education, Anders worked with one of the hospital programmers to create a way to systematically store and retrieve clinical data on patients who were tested on the treadmill—now a common procedure. They also entered data on the coronary angiograms. Anders also wanted to know what happened to patients in the years following the test and planned a research project to collect data to find out. The Long Beach Heart Association, which was at that time very active in fundraising, agreed to support the project for five years. Thus, this created one of the first studies to determine just how useful values collected during treadmill tests might be in predicting cardiac events. A similar study had been reported for the two-step Masters test, but there was no data on the more strenuous exercise test on the treadmill.

Sometime after this was started, Anders heard that Robert Bruce at University of Washington was beginning a similar project in Seattle. Anders visited Bruce and discovered that their exercise protocol, soon to become a standard nationally, was very similar to the one Anders had constructed. Thereafter, the two doctors often compared experiences and ideas.

Within a few years the follow-up data entered in their CDC computer began to indicate that indeed the exercise EKG changes, the heart rate response, and the time on the treadmill all could be used to make clinical predictions about what could happen to the patients. Within a few years the data looked good enough to publish, and for the first time the ST configuration, the time it occurred, the total exercise time, and the heart rate response emerged as useful indicators in patient management. Very soon the same kind of results were published by Bruce in Washington, reconfirming the value of this new way of evaluating patients. For Anders, the publication of this work was followed by invitations to speak nationally and internationally—yet many of the doctors who worked in Long Beach refused to believe that this homegrown product could be of importance and were very reluctant to refer patients.

By 1974, many physicians who had heard Anders' lectures had urged him to write a book, so in 1975 the first edition of *Stress Testing: Principles and Practice* was published by F.A. Davis. The book was a success, which was widely acclaimed, and on the publisher's recommendations it is now in its fifth edition and has been translated into five languages.

Publishing a textbook makes a person an automatic authority, and this drove Anders to live up to others' expectations, just as had been the case in his medical residency in Jersey City when chief resident Carroll Levey had convinced him he could make a difference. He found he could maintain this status but only by continually coming up with new ideas, doing projects to demonstrate the validity of his ideas, and presenting them for peer review and acceptance by the medical community. Although many of his beautiful hypotheses were destroyed by ugly facts, some proved to be valid. Such is the formula for progress.

— TWENTY-FOUR —

DEATH IN THE CATH LAB

Anders had always prided himself on being able to communicate with his patients. He managed this by trying to put himself in their place and by showing how concerned he was for their welfare and their point of view. When he would occasionally lose a patient, he could always deal successfully with the family's loss—well, almost always.

As time passed, the general recognition of the concept of identifying coronary artery disease angiographically and operating to bypass the disease was becoming accepted, which resulted in more and more angiograms and more and more open-heart surgeries.

One day Mort Haskell, a radiologist who was an avid ocean sailor, called Anders about one of his crewmen. Although George was only forty-two years old, he had been having severe chest pain the previous week while they were competing in a race. He had lost his father to a heart attack at age forty-four. Anders agreed to see him, and after only three minutes on the treadmill George developed severe chest pain and an abnormal EKG.

Anders explained to George that he needed an angiogram and probably a coronary bypass operation. He agreed to proceed and they set up a date for the following week. A day before the angiogram was scheduled Anders received a call from George's wife, who seemed almost hysterical. She cried on the phone, exclaiming that she did not want her husband to have the angiogram and saying, "I know you will kill him." Anders tried to reassure her but got nowhere, so he agreed to cancel the procedure.

He then called the patient at work and reiterated the wife's call and said he thought they should cancel the test. George, who was very worried about his heart disease, particularly in view of his father's early death, stated, "Every time I race with Mort I go through this. My wife always cries and claims that she knows I will drown. So I just have to ignore her crazy behavior and live my life. Please let's proceed with the test." Although Anders was somewhat reluctant, he agreed to go ahead and the next morning took George to the cath lab. George appeared in good spirits and signed the consent without even reading it. A mild sedation was administered, the groin was anesthetized, and the femoral artery was cannulated without incident. The catheter was advanced under the fluoroscope and positioned in the opening of the right coronary artery. The camera was started and the contrast agent was injected, just as it had been done hundreds of times before, when suddenly the heart rhythm, which had been stable a minute before, developed ventricular fibrillation.

Cardiac massage was immediately started and electric shock was applied to terminate the abnormal rhythm. One, two, three shocks followed—still, ventricular fibrillation continued. The blood pressure recorded on the monitor was now down to forty millimeters of mercury and an anesthesiologist was called, who immediately introduced an endotracheal catheter to aid in ventilation, now supplied by using an ambou bag. A call went out for a "code blue." The team arrived within minutes and full resuscitation was instituted. Dr. William Bloomer, one of the heart surgeons, responded to see if he could help.

After twenty minutes of resuscitation and numerous electric shocks, a normal rhythm could not be established and it was decided that Bill Bloomer would open the chest and put in a vein bypass to see if it would help. Within an hour this was accomplished, but to no avail. After more than two hours it became obvious that George could not be resuscitated and Anders went out into the hospital lobby to inform George's wife. Upon receiving word that her husband was dead, she started to scream. She threw herself on the floor, screaming, "You killed him. You murderer." Anders did not know what to do. He had reported death to family members before but this was a new experience. He dropped to his knees and tried to console her but she continued to scream, kicking her heels on the carpet. Other people in the hospital lobby gathered around. Some tried to comfort her. Some just stared. It was certainly the worst day in Anders' life. Bill Bloomer, the surgeon who had tried in vain to save the situation, also attempted to console her—with no results. After what seemed like forever she stopped screaming, got up off the floor, and ran out of the lobby.

That night when Anders went home and reported the day's events to his wife, Luci tried in vain to comfort him. The events of the day resulted in extensive reexamination. What went wrong? What could we have done? Needless to say, George's wife did not give consent for an autopsy. In retrospect, the early onset of symptoms on the treadmill suggested that multiple arteries were diseased. Possibly the left main coronary—a notorious common cause of sudden death. They could only guess and hope that such a thing would never happen again. You can be sure that the next time Anders did an angiogram he was pretty anxious.

Two months after that awful day, Anders was served with a subpoena. He was being sued—the lawyers retained by his malpractice insurance carriers decided to settle out of court. Even though there was no evidence that Anders had made any errors and his procedure was within the standard of care and there was no evidence of malpractice, the insurance company decided that if George's wife put on the same kind of screaming act in front of a jury Anders would be doomed.

It was decided that they would settle without going to trial. Anders had no alternative but to go along with his attorneys. Thirty years later, George's wife would approach Anders' wife in a local pie shop, shouting, "I know who you are. Did you know your husband killed my husband? I hope you realize what type of a man he is." Luci's only response was to retreat, hoping she would never run into George's wife again.

This experience generated a good deal of soul searching on Anders' part. He was always depressed after a patient's death. How could he have connected with George's wife and made the terrible event easier for her? That scene in the hospital lobby was forever imprinted on his memory—perhaps even on his soul.

– TWENTY-FIVE –

THE PLAYBOY ARTICLE

Although in his childhood Anders did not think of himself as a rebel, he had grown to admire people who had unconventional ideas. He believed that they were the yeast that leavened the bread. On the other hand, who had ever seen a Chinese person with a "perm"?

Only a few years after starting his fellowship program, which in the early days lasted only a year, Anders accepted George Chung for this position. George had served as a medical resident at Memorial Hospital and Anders recognized him to be energetic, intelligent, and capable even though he was somewhat of a free spirit. George had been born in Hawaii, where his father was a very successful family doctor and a leader in the Chinese American colony of citizens who had established themselves as an important group on the island of Oahu. George's father came to visit Anders at the start of his fellowship to get acquainted with Anders and to explain that George was expected to return to Hawaii to practice in the hospital where his father worked. He explained, "We will have an assured referral base from the Chinese American community there."

As the year progressed Anders realized that although George was bright and hardworking, he was definitely a nonconformist. One day he showed up with curly hair. No one had ever seen a Chinese person with curly hair, and George's "perm" caused a lot of raised eyebrows. Each week on Friday everyone working in cardiology attended a special conference where interesting and controversial cases were presented. One Friday Anders and Chris Manvi, another cardiology fellow, wore fuzzy black wigs and sat down on either side of George in the conference room. The laughter and jokes about George's perm had little effect. When Anders and George went to visit Melvin Judkins at Loma Linda, because he had made quite an impact with his newly designed catheters, Judkins expelled George from his lab. "We don't tolerate girly men in this department." Judkins said a Chinese man with curls was indeed a unique event. Even this did not discourage George.

George confided in Anders that on his weekends off he was experimenting with marijuana and also researching the literature to see if it had any medical applications. Anders pointed out in no uncertain terms that George must not mix marijuana with his work in cardiology. George reassured him that he would not do so.

A few months later George presented Anders with a manuscript describing the medical uses of marijuana. Anders was surprised at the magnitude of George's research of the literature and the apparent logic of his conclusions. Anders made a few minor suggestions but in general approved of the conclusions George had drawn. "Where do you want to submit your manuscript?" Anders asked. "JAMA [Journal of the American Medical Association]," replied George.

So off it went in the mail. Almost three months later George got the bad news. His manuscript had been rejected. Anders was somewhat relieved. He had been apprehensive about the probability that an article of this type might suggest that their institution was promoting the use of marijuana. He soon forgot about the incident, as more important issues were always requiring his attention.

About three months later George approached Anders with a copy of *Playboy* magazine, his eyes beaming with satisfaction. "Look," George said, "they published it in *Playboy*." Anders was surprised beyond words. "You didn't tell me you were submitting it to *Playboy*." "Well," George confessed, "I didn't think you would approve. Also I didn't really think they would print it." All the potential problems related to this publication flashed through Anders' mind. It was clearly stated that the article came from their hospital. Would it be construed that they were suggesting marijuana be used for the treatment of end-stage cancers as George had stated in the article?

The next morning when Anders came into work his secretary announced, "You are requested immediately to report to Don Karner's office." (Don Karner was the chief hospital administrator). Anders' secretary said that Mr. Karner was very upset. Anders had been mulling over how he would deal with this issue. Now he had to face the music. When he walked into Don Karner's office he found not only the administrator but also hospital chief of staff John Lundgren waiting. Neither one looked happy.

Throwing a copy of *Playboy* on the coffee table, John Lundgren said, "Have you seen this magazine?"

Smiling, Anders retorted, "No, it's not one of the journals I regularly read." Then he admitted, "Yes, I am aware of the article."

"Do you want our hospital to be known for promoting marijuana?" Lundgren asked. "How will the staff react? What will the citizens of Long Beach think? What will the Board of Directors say?"

Anders quipped, "Do you think all of these people read *Playboy*?"

"They will read this issue for sure," Don Karner retorted. "We have decided the only thing to do is to fire George Chung and make it clear that the hospital does not condone the use of marijuana."

John Lundgren added, "Then we'll hope the whole thing blows over."

The night before Anders had considered the possibility that this would be proposed. He had been pleased with George's performance as a fellow. He knew that if he was fired it would be almost impossible for him to find another fellowship. He knew what a blow it would be to George's father, who expected George to come back to Hawaii and be the first cardiologist in their community. He decided the night before that he would stick by George, even if it was difficult.

Anders explained to Don Karner and John Lundgren that he reviewed the manuscript, that it was scientifically accurate but that it did not really advocate its use in their hospital. He advised, "If we don't make a big fuss, in a few weeks everyone will forget about it." A few weeks later Anders made the same statement to the Board of Directors, who after a great deal of discussion supported his decision. George, as was his father, was very appreciative of the support Anders had given, and as George's year of training drew to a close Anders too was pleased with himself. Salvaging George's future in cardiology seemed like the right thing to do. George turned out to be an excellent cardiologist, even if he did fail his father by staying in Long Beach after his training was completed rather than returning to Hawaii.

TWENTY-SIX

THE BLOOD BANK
AND HELEN JOHNSON

Open-heart surgery, supported by a heart-lung machine, was first introduced by John Gibon in 1953 after ten years of experimentation. It was soon followed by Walter Lillehei in Minnesota and Ake Senning in Zurich. By the early sixties it was introduced at UCLA and was well-established as the only way to correct many cardiac defects.

In 1965 Anders, Mickey Beland, Harry Orme, Oscar Shadle, and Jerry Cope decided it was time to start an open-heart surgery program at their hospital. Harry, a pediatric cardiologist who had been trained at the University of Minnesota, where an open-heart program had been introduced, was anxious to promote pediatric cardiac surgery. They purchased a disk oxygenator and once a week operated on a dog. Although they loved dogs, it was well-established that any conscientious heart surgeon could not operate on people until he had perfected his technique and equipment on animals.

In the early days of open-heart surgery, the pump oxygenator required ten pints of blood to prime it before it was connected to the patient. The anticoagulant used for all open-heart surgery was Heparin because it had been reported that citrate, the agent commonly used in the blood bank to prevent clotting, was too toxic for this procedure. It was known that citrate prevented clotting by combining with all the calcium in the blood, because calcium was necessary for clotting to take place.

Week after week they repeated the procedure, starting at about 5 p.m. and working until about 10 p.m. They simulated various types of surgery being done at the time—repairing valves and closing defects between the chambers. The dogs that had been operated upon became pets and were given to various hospital personnel. One of the nurses from the O.R., Frances Weiss, volunteered to help and eventually inherited the chore of cleaning the heart-lung machine. Soon thereafter she became the nurse manager of the fledgling department of Clinical Physiology, soon to be renamed Cardiology. After each run, the disks had to be washed in acid to remove the protein from the previous case.

After six months of work they decided it was time to do a real case, and a thirty-two-year-old woman with an atrial septal defect (a hole between the upper chambers of the heart) was selected. When she did well they all knew their preparations had paid off and that they could call themselves a successful open-heart surgery team. In the next few years they established their program in the community, and open-heart cases no longer had to be referred to UCLA, who had started a program several years earlier.

One of the biggest challenges in doing a case was obtaining enough blood to prime the pump oxygenator. Because blood was collected in Heparin, which was a poor preservative, five or six donors had to be assembled the day before the case. This precluded doing a case as an emergency and members of the open-heart team decided that there must be some way to safely use the citrated blood from the blood bank. Accordingly, each Monday night the routine of doing dog surgery was again established. This time Corinne Monroe and Elmer Jennings, from the blood bank, also contributed.

The animals were put on the heart-lung machine and then infused with larger and larger doses of citrate, the agent used in the blood bank to prevent clotting. As the citrate concentrations increased and the dogs progressively became decalcified, all of their muscles ceased to contract including their diaphragm, which was responsible for breathing, and they could only be kept alive by artificial ventilation. If, however, they were supported by the heart-lung machine for about one hour longer, their blood calcium amazingly returned toward normal. It turned out that the calcium from the bones was surprisingly mobile, and served as a reservoir that replenished the calcium that had been removed from the blood by the citrate. The doctors then used citrated blood and added a second anticoagulant, Heparin. Following this they added enough calcium to combine with all the citrate. Using this mixture to prime the pump, they found it did not decalcify the dogs. Indeed, it worked just as well as the blood that had been drawn in Heparin originally. They were elated—now they could use citrated banked blood, add Heparin and calcium, and not have to collect blood in Heparin from the large group of volunteers from the night before.

About the time they became convinced they had discovered a way to used banked blood for open-heart surgery, an incident occurred that crystallized their thinking. Dr. Caraco had a patient named Helen Johnson, who was in severe heart failure because of advanced mitral insufficiency (a leaky mitral valve). As was his habit before he left for the desert on Friday afternoon, he called Anders and asked him to hospitalize Mrs. Johnson because her heart failure was becoming uncontrollable. When Anders examined her, her lungs were full of fluid, and it was his opinion that she was not going to make it. She needed an artificial valve inserted.

No one in Long Beach had done this kind of surgery but a pioneering surgeon from Portland, Albert Star, had recently reported success with a caged ball device that was being made for him by a retired engineer in his garage not far from Long Beach. A call to the engineer, Mr. Edwards, revealed that he had a few valves but they needed to have a sewing ring attached. He said he would go out and get the girl who would attach the sewing ring, and if someone would come to his garage at about 9 p.m. that night it would be ready.

Anders assembled the surgeons and, for the first time in a human patient, Frances Weiss primed the pump with banked blood. Helen's husband was dispatched to Edwards' garage to pick up the valve. At about 10 p.m. he returned to the hospital, where the valve was sterilized and by midnight had been sewed into the mitral ring of Helen's heart. By 1 a.m. the surgery was over, Helen's lungs were no longer full of fluid, and by morning she was sitting up in bed breathing easier. Everyone was elated, including Helen, her husband, Anders, Mickey Beland, Harry Orme, and Frances Weiss. What a night! The first emergency open-heart, the first use of banked blood, and a much-improved patient.

A few days later Harry Orme reported that, unbeknownst to those working with Anders, the team at UCLA had also arrived at the same conclusion and had been using banked blood for more than a month. Even so, everyone was elated with their achievement and sometime later published their results.

Helen did well for several years, though her husband and she separated. He claimed that her valve made so much noise that he couldn't sleep. She remained a loyal patient of Anders for twenty years and finally died of breast cancer.

The open-heart surgery program continued to prosper, and within a few years was the recognized leader in the Harbor area.

TWENTY-SEVEN

THE REDHEAD AND THE PREACHER

A nders' wife, Luci, the daughter of a Methodist minister in Kentucky, believed that attending church was very important. As their family grew, Anders, Luci, and the kids became regulars at the California Heights Methodist Church. Luci taught Sunday School and Anders sang in the choir, an activity he enjoyed immensely. A few years after they joined, a new young preacher, Paul Woudenberg, was assigned to the church and immediately became very popular. Anders, too, admired him a great deal. Despite their activities in the church, Luci and Anders drifted farther apart. It seemed as though they disagreed on everything. Paul Woudenberg tried to broker some sort of understanding between the two, but his attempt failed. After thirteen years of marriage Luci filed for divorce, and after a few months the divorce was completed.

Anders moved out of the house and into an apartment, which was in the same apartment house as the preacher, who had never married. Many times over the following year Anders would come back to his apartment after evening rounds and he and Paul would have extensive philosophical discussions that were wide-ranging and very stimulating. Having studied engineering at Cal Tech prior to attending divinity school, Paul Woudenberg was unusually intelligent for a preacher, Anders thought.

Sometimes when Anders took his older kids, who were now in high school, skiing, Paul Woudenberg accompanied them to Mammoth, where they enjoyed their camaraderie. Paul Woudenberg even asked Anders to preach a sermon one Sunday, which Anders enjoyed a great deal, although his topic, "The Psychological Need to Suffer," didn't go over very well with the congregation. During this time, as he sat in the choir, Anders noticed a strikingly beautiful redhead, who attended church regularly. When he asked Paul about her, Paul told him, "That's Mira Carter, a very successful fashion model, who has become a regular here at Cal Heights."

Anders remarked, "It's about time you married, Paul. She looks like she would be a perfect wife."

"Sorry," Paul answered. "Although her husband never attends church, she seems happily married."

As the first year of Anders' single life wore on he realized that not having a wife was pretty lonely. Although he occasionally dated, he recognized he was not cut out to be a swinging bachelor. Interestingly, one evening as he and Paul were engaged in some deep discussion, Paul suddenly changed the subject. "You remember the redhead, Mira Carter, who comes to church? Well, she has recently become a widow. Her husband died suddenly last week."

"Golly," Anders retorted, "what happened?"

"I'm not sure," Paul answered, "but he had been ailing for several months."

Anders had heard something to the effect that he had been in the hospital several times. "She has three children," Paul explained, "but I think you would like her and I really think you need a wife."

Anders pondered the issue for a while and finally agreed. "How soon do you think it would be appropriate to call her?"

"Three months," Paul decided.

That night Anders got out his appointment book and wrote himself a reminder, although he really didn't need the book. The three months seemed like an eternity. During this period it was rumored around Cal Heights Church that Paul was helping Mira readjust to being without a husband, and Anders wondered if Paul had suggested a three-month wait so that he could get in on the ground floor.

When the time came, Anders called Mira and suggested they go out to dinner. When he came by to pick her up he was introduced to her three children and shown through their home, which, though modest in size, was in a nice neighborhood and neat as a pin. A year later, they married. Anders thought the union was made in heaven. After all, it had been orchestrated by his pastor, who was also an intimate friend by now.

Mira and Anders decided the wedding should be private and, because Anders' and Mira's children went to school together, it would be better if they didn't attend the ceremony, although Cal Heights Church was only a few blocks from where Mira lived and only half a mile from the house where Anders' family resided. They decided Paul Woudenberg would do the honors with only a few people in attendance. Mira's parents and sister were included.

When the brief ceremony was over and they exited the church, all of Anders' and Mira's children were sitting on the steps. As the newlyweds exited the church, the kids all threw rice and vowed they would all be one big happy family. Such was the start of a marriage that would be the best thing that ever happened to Anders. When Anders adopted Mira's three children, the judge reminded them that although Anders would be their new father and their last name would now be Erickssen, and that he would take good care of them, they had to realize that someday he would get old and they would have to care for him. The judge wanted to know if they agreed to this arrangement. The unexpected aspect of this adoption caused a few moments of doubt, but after looking at each other with a degree of uncertainty the kids agreed. They later admitted that after thinking about it for a few minutes they decided it was probably so distant they didn't have to worry. Anders moved into Mira's home, and within a few months Anders' oldest daughter, Bonnie, joined them after being ousted by her mother. It was a crowded and lively household.

With his new marriage, Anders' social status in medical circles and in the community went up a notch or two. He found that being married to a very beautiful woman produced considerable admiration and possibly a little envy among his peers. Mira was not only supportive of all of Anders' medical activities, regardless of their profitability, but also took up skiing and tennis, which they enjoyed together in the few times that Anders was away from his professional duties. Thus, a romance had been initiated that both expected to endure far into the future.

— TWENTY-EIGHT —

LIMA, PERU

The year after his marriage to Mira, Anders was invited to make a presentation at an international cardiology conference in Lima, Peru. His work in exercise testing was resulting in a number of international speaking engagements, which he enjoyed immensely. He not only had a chance to meet outstanding physicians from foreign countries but the other speakers were also usually influential cardiologists from the U.S., resulting in many lasting friendships for Anders.

One evening in Lima Anders was invited to a reception, where he was seated with Conrad Klinnert, a heart surgeon from Munich, Germany, with whom he had become acquainted a few years earlier. Klinnert explained to Anders and Mira that Christian Barnard, who had just become world famous for performing the first heart transplant, was going to join them. Conrad told them that he and Barnard had trained together at the University of Minnesota, where they both had learned how to do transplants on dogs under the tutelage of Norman Shumway. He confided to Anders that it was too bad that Barnard was getting so much credit because Shumway, who was now at Stanford, was really the "father" of heart transplants.

Shortly after giving this explanation, Barnard appeared

escorting a strikingly beautiful young girl. During the introduction Barnard, who was very handsome himself, explained that his lady friend had recently been crowned Miss World at an international beauty contest. Laughingly, he said, "Conrad, do you remember when we were in Minnesota and used to go out looking for girls? Since I've done the first transplant, the girls are now looking for me." Indeed, it appeared to everyone that he was being treated like a rock star.

Mira was unimpressed. After Barnard and his girlfriend had circulated to other tables, Mira reminded Anders and Conrad that Barnard had a wife and children back in Cape Town, South Africa. "Why isn't his wife here to share all of his accolades?"

The next night, Anders and Mira were invited to a show at one of Lima's most prestigious cabarets. In the party was Mason Sones from Cleveland, a famous heart surgeon and his wife from Houston, and Pablo Zubiati—a Peruvian heart surgeon—who had met Anders when taking his training in the U.S. After they had eaten a sumptuous dinner and several entertainers had performed, a very sexy, black dancer came on the stage. She gyrated through a quite suggestive dance called the Marinara. The music temporarily stopped. The dancer then ran to Anders' party's table and grabbed the heart surgeon from Houston's hand, pulling him up onto the stage. The music resumed and she taught him how to do the dance with her, much to his wife's apparent dismay.

After a few minutes the surgeon's wife leaned over to Mira and remarked, "I do declare, I believe that's the first time he has ever danced with a Negro." Anders thought, *You can take the girl out of the South but you can't take the South out of the girl.* Mira and Anders never forgot this gala or the comments of the surgeon's wife, who truly was a Southern Belle.

The next morning the group flew to Cuzco, 11,000 feet in the Andes, followed the next day by a train ride to Machu

Picchu. Machu Picchu was an ancient Incan city discovered in 1911 by Hiram Bingham from Yale. Perched on a mountain in the middle of the jungle, it was probably never found by the Spanish conquistadors who conquered the Inca. It is believed to have been built in the fifteenth century.

Mason Sones found the thin air at Cuzco and Machu Picchu to be too much for a chain-smoker. He never made it from the train station up the trail to the ruins in Machu Picchu. Anders was relieved to see that Sones, whose lips were slightly blue and who was laboring for breath, finally made it back to the airport at Cuzco. When he descended to Lima at sea level, where there was more oxygen, he was much relieved. On the plane back to the U.S. they all agreed, with the exception of Mason Sones, that everything in Peru was wonderful, especially the dancing of the Marinara. The group joked to the Houston surgeon's wife that he had really missed his calling.

TWENTY-NINE

DR. TRUCKLER

As the cardiology program grew and became more complex, Anders found he was giving his fellows in training more and more responsibility. Although they provided a service to the cardiologists who worked in the heart program, the fact that their performance remained at a high level was, for Anders, a source of pride. As it turned out, when they finished their training, many stayed in Long Beach and became outstanding cardiologists, bringing credit to the program. Many also went to the other cities in the Los Angeles Basin, where they spread the word that Memorial Hospital's program was of high caliber.

This made the selection of each new fellow a very serious enterprise. Fortunately, affiliation with the UCI Medical School resulted in a datapool of good candidates from which to choose. One year, as Anders was pondering whom to select, he got a call from a cardiologist in New York recommending one of his internal medicine residents who wished to come to California for his training. This medical resident was touted as extremely bright and industrious and, after reading the many letters of recommendation and reviewing his medical school transcript, Anders was convinced he would fit right in and be a trainee of whom they could all be proud. Anders accepted him without an interview, which he had never done before.

The new resident arrived on July 1st, right on schedule, and Anders was convinced he had made a good choice. Truckler was a short, stocky redhead with a very serious demeanor, which Anders took to mean he would be industrious, sincere, and reliable. Truckler's medical school transcript testified that he was academically superior. As was the usual practice, he was assigned to the catheterization laboratory the first week, where he would write a history and physical on each patient coming in for the procedure and scrub with the attending cardiologist. All was well for about three weeks, but then Anders began to hear complaints from the nurses and technicians working with him. They reported that Truckler was surly, very critical of their performance, and often rude to the patients. Anders had failed to see this when scrubbing with Truckler, but the nurses said, "He's on his good behavior when you're in the room." Soon he began to treat the nurses and techs abusively, sometimes accusing them of incidents that were completely imaginary.

Anders' discussion with Truckler about these claims was completely unproductive. Truckler denied all the accusations and made it clear that two of the nurses were "out to get him." Soon some of the cardiologists were telling Anders that they refused to have him scrub with them. This was heretofore an unheard of situation at Memorial Hospital. One day Bill Wilson, the chief of radiology, who frequently took part in the catheterizations, announced to Anders that Truckler could never again work in the same laboratory with him—that he was not only incompetent, but sometimes also completely off the wall in his outbursts. Anders again discussed these issues with Truckler and decided to remove him from the cath lab and have him work in the treadmill lab. He assigned him to cover the intensive care unit during his night call.

Anders didn't know why Truckler was having so much trouble,

but from his conversations decided that Truckler was very insecure and at times inappropriate in his behavior. He decided that Truckler would require a lot of mentoring and Anders committed himself to spending extra time bringing him around. Several of the cardiologists who had worked with Truckler told Anders, "You should get rid of him. You picked a bad apple." By now, Truckler had worked at Memorial Hospital for three months. Although he was well-informed and seemed industrious enough, almost all of the nurses were complaining. Some told Anders, "We think he's a little nuts."

Truckler was living in an apartment owned by the hospital just across the parking lot, and he found this very convenient when he had to respond to late night calls from the intensive care ward. One morning, after Truckler had been up a good deal of the night taking calls, a worker repairing a broken sewer line in the parking lot started a jackhammer at about 8 a.m., just outside of Truckler's window. Truckler awoke, pulled on a bathrobe, and ran outside pointing a pistol at the workman. "If you don't stop that noise, I'll blow your damn brains out." The worker dropped the jackhammer and ran for his life. About half an hour later the workman and a local policeman came to Anders' office in the hospital. "Doctor, you've got a wild man in your department," they said.

Anders was shocked. He and the policeman went to Truckler's apartment, where, after a screaming episode of obscene language from Truckler, he finally agreed to give up his pistol. It was indeed loaded. Truckler was taken to jail and booked on the charge of threatening with a deadly weapon. Anders spent a couple of hours discussing the episode with Truckler and came to believe that Truckler might be hallucinating. Anders was now convinced that he was dealing with a barely compensated schizophrenic.

The next day, Truckler was released on bail and Anders called a meeting of all the cardiologists working at the hospital. It was agreed that Truckler had to be terminated. It was obvious to everyone that he had no insight into his problem. When Anders informed Truckler that his fellowship had to be terminated, Truckler went into a tirade. "You'll be sorry you've done this to me." As he was being threatened, Anders visualized Truckler coming after him with a gun. If he would threaten a worker who woke him up, what would he do to a man who had "ruined his career"?

A month after Truckler was gone Anders was served with a notice that a lawsuit had been filed against him and the hospital administration. Although Don Karner, the administrator, appreciated some of the credits Anders had brought to the hospital, he decided that some of his trainees were getting to be a pain. He reminded Anders about the problem with George Chung a few years before. Anders requested that the hospital foot the bill for the legal defense. This resulted in a special meeting of the Board of Directors, where the majority was of the opinion that Anders had gotten himself into this by recruiting a nut. Fortunately one Board member, a very influential attorney in town, convinced them that it was the hospital's duty to defend Anders as well as the hospital itself against this crazy, legal action.

The case dragged on for two years. Every time Anders was required to appear, he was half-afraid Truckler might come armed. Truckler made it clear that he continued to be very angry, but as the case dragged on Anders began to realize that his chances of being shot during these hearings were diminishing. After two years, a judge threw the suit out of court, and the ordeal was over.

Never again did Anders accept a trainee without an interview, although he often pondered whether he would have been able to detect Truckler's problem. It seems unlikely. One thing was certain—running a cardiology program was never dull.

THIRTY

MARV TRADNOR

If you were a doctor, would you treat a man who murdered your best friend? The practice of medicine is not just having the knowledge and skills to take care of the sick. Difficult moral and ethical discussions are fairly common. For example, do you spend hours of your time and thousands of dollars of your hospital's money treating a patient who abuses himself and others around him when you could spend these resources on a deserving citizen? This difficult dilemma is illustrated by what was, for Anders, an agonizing experience.

When Anders began to establish his practice in Long Beach, he felt the need to take part in the community and become acquainted with young businessmen who were outside the medical profession. To accomplish this he joined the Junior Chamber of Commerce. He soon learned that much of the activity took place in some of the committees, and he discovered that the Public Relations Committee was populated by some of the young men who were the most active in the community. Although most of those on the committee were either lawyers or real estate brokers, Anders enjoyed the interchange and soon became accepted as a contributing activist. They even appointed him committee chairman. The Public Relations Committee was very involved in city politics and especially in the behavior of the chief of police, who was believed by members of the committee to be quite corrupt.

Anders became close friends with one member, Marv Tradnor, who practiced law with his father, a very prestigious Long Beach attorney. Marv was one of the few attorneys Anders had met whom he believed to be uncharacteristically honest. Until meeting Marv, Anders had lumped most attorneys into the same category as Melvin Belli. Here was a man who convinced Anders that there were many lawyers who were indeed good citizens, and he was pleased to call Marv his friend.

The two friends decided that if Anders ever needed legal advice Marv Tradnor would provide it and, in exchange, when Marv needed advice on medical matters, Anders would provide it—all at no cost. The interchange worked out well. In years to follow when Marv had a client with a medical complaint he could obtain an opinion from Anders that he could count on, and when Anders had legal problems his friendship with Marv turned out to be invaluable.

About ten years after the friends had met, Marv's domestic bliss evaporated, and after a difficult divorce he started dating a young woman who had recently divorced her orthopedic surgeon husband, Brad Alitori. When Marv confided in Anders about his attraction Anders approved, as he had met the couple on a number of ski trips where a group of doctors had come together for skiing, medical education, and social discourse. When Marv discussed his relationship with Marge, Anders told him that he had often wondered if her marriage to Brad would last, considering the disagreements he was aware of from some of their social interactions.

Many years later, after the liaison turned tragic, Anders wondered what would have happened if he had discouraged his friend's interest in Marge.

Within a year of his divorce, Brad Alitori remarried but continued to come by and take his children on outings, two or three times a month. One Sunday afternoon, Brad and his new wife came by Marge's house when Marv Tradnor was visiting. Brad rang the doorbell and said he planned to take the kids to Knott's Berry Farm for dinner. Marge retorted that this was not his regular day for visitation and he couldn't take them. Because of Brad's obscene shouting, Marge asked him to go into the kitchen so they could settle their argument privately. Marv and the children stayed in the living room. However, the shouting was clearly audible, in spite of the closed doors. Suddenly there was a scream. Marv and the children rushed into the kitchen and to their horror saw that Brad had slashed Marge's throat and abdomen with a butcher knife. Marv rushed to her defense and within a few minutes both he and Marge lay dead, cut to pieces in a pool of blood. The screams of his children and his own sobbing intermingled as Brad realized he had just committed a double murder in front of his children. He ran to the phone and called 911.

The following day, Anders discovered the news of his friend's death by reading the headlines in the newspaper. He was crushed. He could do nothing but attend Marv's funeral, where many of their friends from the Junior Chamber of Commerce testified to Marv's service to the community and to his reputation as an outstanding member of the legal profession.

Brad Alitori served ten years for double murder. As years passed Anders rarely thought about the incident but never forgot about Marv and the murder.

– TWENTY YEARS LATER –

One morning at 9 a.m. Anders came to the office and looked over the list of patients for the day. As usual, they were scheduled at fifteen-minute intervals with the last one, a new patient, scheduled for forty-five minutes. Looking over the list, Anders was shocked. There on his patient list was the name "Brad Alitori." For the next three hours as he was seeing his usual patients, he agonized over how to handle his last appointment of the day. Should he refuse to see the man who had murdered one of his best friends? Many memories flashed through his mind. His first impulse was to have his receptionist turn Brad away. Anders then thought he should excoriate Brad for what he had done. Anders wondered if Brad even knew of Anders' relationship with Marv Tradnor.

When the difficult three hours had passed and the time arrived for the meeting, Anders decided to lay his case on the line. He began, "Hi Brad, it's been a long time since I've seen you, as you well know. When I saw your name on the patient list today it created an emotional conflict of major proportions. You probably didn't know this, but Marv Tradnor was one of my very closest friends. I was, needless to say, furious, devastated, and speechless when you did him in. I've agonized all morning as to whether I should accept you as a patient. I finally decided that I would hear what you have to say."

Brad responded, "No, I didn't know he was your friend. I can only say, as you well know, that I did a terrible thing in a fit of rage. I've had to live with this and will for the rest of my life. I went to prison and have paid my debt to society. I made my peace with my kids. We are now completely reconciled. I have a cardiac problem and I respect your judgment more than anyone else's. I need you as my doctor. I ask for your forgiveness. Please accept me as a patient." Tears were running down his cheeks.

At that moment Anders decided, due to something he could not explain, that it would be the right thing to do.

It turned out that Brad had chronic atrial fibrillation (an irregular heartbeat) but his heart was otherwise normal, and with appropriate medication followed by electrocardioversion (an electric shock) his rhythm returned to normal and he became a regular patient in the ensuing years. As the years went by, Anders often reexamined his decision but always came to the same conclusion—he believed he had done the right thing.

THIRTY-ONE

TRAGEDY ON THE COURT

W hen the interchange between a doctor and a patient is analyzed, what is the responsibility of the doctor? Of the patient? If patients fail to follow the advice of the doctor is he to blame when the treatment fails? Is the court the best place to adjudicate this problem? How do social pressures, the feelings of the family and community, factor into the problem?

One morning as Anders scanned the newspaper, the headlines announced the unthinkable—Henry Gather, a Loyola College basketball star who led the nation in both scoring and rebounding, had dropped dead during a game with dozens of pro scouts looking on. The article went on to tell that Gather had been under a doctor's care and had played with his permission. Needless to say the article was pretty critical of the medical profession for allowing this outstanding African American basketball player, with an almost assured future in the NBA, to die during the game.

For the next week, the paper ran stories on the failed attempt at resuscitation, questioning whether Gather should have been allowed to play, why he could not be resuscitated, and what his coaches and friends had to say about his death. The press implied that someone would have to pay for the mistakes made. They were correct. Within a few weeks lawsuits were filed against the university, the doctor who had been treating Gather, the team doctors, and the orthopedic resident who happened to be at the game and happened to be involved in the attempted resuscitation.

It turned out that Gather had passed out during practice a few months earlier and Dr. Hatori, an electrophysiologist, had diagnosed ventricular tachycardia (a very serious cardiac irregularity). He believed the rhythm might be controlled with the medication Inderal, a beta blocker that tends to insulate the heart from adrenalin and other similar hormones. After the medication was instituted, they had Gather wear a holter monitor (a tape recorded electrocardiogram) to monitor his rhythm while he played in a practice game. The test was a success. If he took the medicine regularly it appeared that the onset of VT could be prevented. He returned to the team and continued for several months to be the leading scorer. Gather, the coach, and Gather's mother were all elated. His expected career in the NBA was still on track.

Beta blockers, while they protect some patients from arrhythmias, have side effects. They slow the heart rate and reduce the maximum cardiac output (heart pumping capacity), which Gather was conscious of. He was aware that he got more tired and had to sit out more than before, and he discovered on his own that if he took half of the prescribed dose he could function better. He called Dr. Hatori and complained. It was agreed, according to the testimony, that he could try half the dose for this very important game, where Gather knew there would be several pro scouts watching. He wanted to be at his best for this special occasion and was confident he would be okay without the full dose.

Much to everyone's horror he collapsed during the game, and, when he was examined by the volunteer physician, it appeared that Gather had had a cardiac arrest. Closed chest massage was started immediately and within a few minutes the coach brought out a defibrillator, which the university had purchased after

Gather had developed his problem. Although his training in orthopedics did not fully qualify him for cardiac resuscitation with an electrical defibrillator, the orthopedic resident did his best but to no avail. They finally dragged Gather off the court and eventually into an ambulance. By the time he was placed in the ambulance it was reported that his lungs were full of fluid, and after a short ride to the hospital he was pronounced dead.

A few weeks later it was announced that the insurance company for the university, and the one covering Dr. Hatori, had agreed to settle on the losses for one million dollars. As the news stories continued to document the events, Anders received a call from the attorney defending the orthopedic resident. It was his opinion that he did everything he could and should not be found guilty of malpractice. Anders agreed to serve as expert witness and received all the evidence available. The body had been taken to the County Coroner's office, where an autopsy had been done. Anders traveled to Los Angeles and met with the coroner, who told him that the underlying heart problem was myocarditis. Anders wanted to see for himself. He examined the heart, which appeared on the surface to be fairly normal, and then reviewed the microscopic slides. Although Anders was a cardiologist and not a pathologist, his year in pathology in San Francisco County Hospital had given him more familiarity with pathology than most cardiologists had. Anders thought the microscopic slides looked more like what he had seen in people who died after an overdose of cocaine. He knew that cocaine use was not unusual in outstanding athletes and asked the coroner about it, who replied, "If you think I am going to agree with you and label this kid who is a folk hero to his friends as a cocaine user, you're crazy."

Anders came away believing he was probably correct and, a week later, while he was being deposed by the plaintiff's attorney, he testified about his belief in the cause of death. The attorney looked shocked. He went off the record and took the defense attorney out of the room for a conference. It was never explained to Anders exactly what transpired in this conference. The trial was set for the following week.

On the morning Anders was scheduled to go to Los Angeles for the trial and be deposed in front of the court, he got a call with the news, "The trial is over." The family fired their attorney and the judge declared no trial. The family had fired Mr. Flegle, who, by the way, was both an attorney and an M.D., because his fees were outrageous.

In the weeks following the trial, Anders' deposition was made part of the public record. When his testimony was reviewed by the press he received several irate phone calls from reporters about his belief that the basketball star's problem was due to cocaine.

Over the next several months, when Anders described the slides to some of his friends who had experience with cocaine hearts, some agreed that he was probably right and some claimed that they couldn't be sure. Anders also knew that he couldn't be sure. Although he felt that he was probably right about the diagnosis, he recognized that it was not politically correct to say so. He guessed he would never know for sure. Discussions about Henry Gather would go on for years.

As Anders reanalyzed the events he concluded that the coroner had a point, that it would be a blow to Gather's family and friends. Yet maybe going public with the cocaine story might have influenced other athletes and saved lives in the future. Who can tell?

― THIRTY-TWO ―

GEORGE HART AND
HYPERBARIC OXYGEN

The Naval Hospital in Long Beach was the home to a very
active hyperbaric oxygen program spearheaded by George
Hart, an international authority in this field. "Hyperbaric
oxygen" means that the pressure under which it is delivered is
high, usually three times atmospheric. In its beginning, this
modality was developed for use in the bends, the release of
nitrogen bubbles in the bloodstream, a complication of deep sea
diving. It was also found to be of value in chronic infection,
wound healing, carbon monoxide poisoning, and other condi-
tions. Anders' senior partner, Elleston Farrell, developed a
cerebral embolus to broca's area in the brain, leaving him aphasic
(unable to speak). Hoping the oxygen under three atmospheres of
pressure would favor a recovery, Anders called Dr. Hart. It was
arranged for Dr. Farrell to have treatments at the Navy Hospital
under Dr. Hart's supervision. This resulted in a complete recovery.

Because of the successful result, when the Navy decided to close
the hospital Anders was one of the physicians who supported the
moving of the hyperbaric program to Memorial Hospital. Dr. Hart
retired from the Navy and transferred his activities, where he soon
found he had a thriving program, primarily treating stubborn
wound infections. It turned out that this treatment favored rapid

healing when the patient was treated with a two-hour session of three atmospheres of pressure under 100 percent oxygen. One morning, while driving to work, Dr. Hart experienced a crushing chest pain that almost stopped him in mid-commute. He prevailed, however, and arrived a few minutes later at the hospital emergency department, where an EKG revealed an acute anterior myocardial infarction (heart attack).

After placing a call for a cardiologist, Hart decided to go upstairs and put himself in a hyperbaric chamber. Within a few minutes after he had come up to three atmospheres of pressure his pain subsided. About one hour later he was persuaded by his cardiologist to leave the chamber, whereby the chest pain returned, although it was much less severe. A nitroglycerine drip was started along with TPA, a thrombolytic (a clot buster), and Heparin, which resulted in resolution of the EKG changes and the evolution of the sizeable myocardial infarction. Within a month he was back at work and urging Anders to put together a clinical trial combining hyperbaric oxygen and R-TPA.

Soon thereafter, Hart was describing an animal study just completed by his friend Paul Thomas in Cleveland, Ohio. The combination of hyperbaric oxygen and TPA in dogs appeared to dramatically reduce the size of an infarct, and after Anders visited Dr. Thomas he was convinced they should put together a study. Genentech, who manufactured TPA, agreed to fund the project. Within a month, they had rigged a hyperbaric chamber with a way to monitor blood pressure and the electrocardiogram, as well as to infuse TPA while they increased the atmospheric pressure to three atmospheres and the patient breathed 100 percent oxygen.

When the first patient was treated, it was truly an event. The patient was placed in a chamber with glass ports, and Anders, George Hart, and other members of the team watched with anticipation while they increased the pressure to three atmospheres and monitored the electrocardiogram. Fifteen minutes after the patient had reached pressure he reported that his chest pain was improving, and a few minutes later the ST elevation on the electrocardiogram, which characterizes an acute myocardial infarction, began to subside. Within half an hour the pain was gone and the ST elevation was markedly improved. "Just like I predicted," George exalted to Anders. "We have a winner!"

Over the next year sixty-six patients were enrolled, half receiving TPA without hyperbaric oxygen and half with the active ingredient. Not all were as successful as the first one, but the hyperbaric oxygen patients had a better ejection fraction (a measure of left ventricular function) and a reduced infarct size as estimated by the CPK (a blood test to measure the amount of heart muscle death).

About the time the good results were being announced several centers began to report the use of angioplasty to open the obstructed artery. The excellent results reported in several centers in the U.S. and Europe, combined with the fact that only a few hospitals had hyperbaric chambers, resulted in the near total abandonment of hyperbaric oxygen as a treatment for an acute myocardial infarction, even though George and Anders believed it could be combined with angioplasty to good effect.

A few years later, George and Anders, sharing lunch in the doctors' dining room, bemused over how excited they had been that first day, in the belief that they had made a major breakthrough in reducing the amount of injury in patients with a heart attack. Even in their own hospital this treatment had been completely abandoned. Anders reported, however, that it was still being used in Belgrade, Yugoslavia, where they had never introduced angioplasty for an acute MI because they were getting such good results with TPA and hyperbaric oxygen. George said, "Well, that proves we made a difference, even if it was only appreciated in Belgrade."

Sixteen years later (in 2004) a speaker at the annual Cutting Edge Symposium at Memorial described the use of an aqueous hyperbaric infusion into the myocardium after the coronary artery had been opened by angioplasty. He reported that the work published by George Hart and Anders had stimulated him to devise this new way to combine hyperbaric oxygen with PTCA. He was very enthusiastic about the preliminary results. The following week, again in the doctors' dining room, Anders remarked to George Hart, "Maybe we made a difference in the U.S. as well as in Yugoslavia."

– THIRTY-THREE –

THE FAA

One thing Anders learned over the years is that politics and federal bureaucracy don't always work perfectly to protect public safety. On the other hand, there are many conscientious people in government, and in the long run the public is well served. Anders' experience with the FAA illustrates some of the problems.

In 1972, the data collection on patients who had a treadmill stress test was beginning to pay off. Anders' team of investigators, funded by the Long Beach Heart Association, had assembled follow-up data on almost 3,000 subjects who had been tested on the treadmill, thus confirming their belief that one could use this test to predict cardiac events in the future. The Federal Air Surgeon, who was the chief of the medical division of the FAA, believed this test might be useful to predict which commercial pilots with suspected heart disease might be a risk to aviation safety if they returned to the cockpit. Thus, he recruited Anders as a consultant. This required Anders to fly to Washington, D.C., for a meeting every two months. The consulting group consisted of two or three cardiologists and neurologists, an orthopedic surgeon, and a psychiatrist. They acted as an advisory board to the Federal Air Surgeon, reviewing case histories and clinical information on pilots who had had heart attacks and other types of disabilities, to determine the potential risks of allowing them to resume flying.

Anders enjoyed this trip immensely and boned up on everything he could find on aviation medicine. The other consultants were all outstanding experts in their field, and they soon developed a camaraderie and friendship that would last for years.

By 1980 ALPA (Airline Pilots Association), the pilots' union, was pushing to abolish the Age Sixty Rule, which would allow commercial pilots to continue to work after this age, which had been prohibited by the FAA for fifteen years. Anders believed that if they underwent an appropriate battery of tests, including a treadmill test, modifying this rule would not compromise aviation safety. His testimony before a congressional fact-finding committee attracted a good deal of national discussion, which led to the ACC (American College of Cardiology) convening a "Bethesda Conference" on the subject, with Anders as the chairman of the cardiology section.

About the time the scientific and political climate seemed ready to alter the Age Sixty Rule, ALPA suddenly reversed their position and opposed the change. As it turned out, the enormous increase in commercial aviation that occurred in the eighties resulted in the balance of power in ALPA switching from the "old pilots to the young pilots." The young pilots wanted the old pilots to retire, thus allowing for their seniority to accrue to the younger ones. This would result in better pay and more freedom to select the favored routes. Under the ALPA pressure Congress abandoned the move to change the Age Sixty Rule, which is still in force today. In 1984, H.L. Reighart, M.D., the Federal Air Surgeon, abandoned the move to change the Age Sixty Rule and retired. Shortly thereafter, a new Federal Air Surgeon, Frank Adams, was appointed.

Dr. Adams, after finishing his internship, joined the Navy and became a naval flight surgeon. He then abandoned medicine and became a line pilot, flying off carriers in World War II and thereafter until he was deemed too old for combat flying. He then reverted to being a doctor and worked in the Aerospace Center in Houston, Texas, prior to his appointment to the role of Federal Air Surgeon.

The first consultants' meeting after Adams' appointment was somewhat of a shock to Anders and the other consultants. Dr. Adams greeted the group, most of whom by this time had served for over ten years, with a new dictum. He informed them that he knew more about aviation medicine than all of the consultants put together, and he didn't intend to follow their advice, as his predecessor had. The consultants reminded him that medicine had made enormous advancements since he finished his internship and the very specialties represented on the consultants' panel had special knowledge necessary to determine who was safe to fly. Adams said that was a lot of bunk and he would call consultants' panels when he needed them, but it probably wouldn't be too often.

Anders and the other consultants were stunned. Within a few months the staff at the Federal Air Surgeon's office were calling Anders and the other consultants to report that Adams was releasing many pilots to return to flying who had been previously rejected by the panel. They reported that any pilot, regardless of his cardiac status, could take Adams out to lunch and come away with an exemption that would allow him to be a first officer on a commercial airline 747. The FAA staff was fearful that before long there would be an in-flight catastrophe because some pilot with a bad heart would bring down the plane.

Anders wrote a letter outlining his concerns and those of the other consultants, which was never answered. Finally, after a few months, Anders submitted his resignation from the consultants' panel with a long explanation justifying his actions. He copied the letter to some of the other consultants, but this seemed somewhat futile because Adams had abolished the panel by then. By 1985, complaints were coming in from everywhere.

The medical officer of Continental Airlines, Robert Wicke, M.D., who was also the president of the Airline Medical Director's Association, complained, "Adams' policies could result in a 747 cockpit with as many as sixteen bypasses." This meant that the pilot, the copilot, and the navigator might previously have had cardiac surgery with five or six vein bypass grafts implanted. It was well-known that it was not uncommon for these grafts to close soon after surgery, resulting in an insufficient blood flow to the heart. On August 3rd of 1985, Joseph O'Brien, a corporate helicopter pilot with severe heart disease, who had recently been released to fly by Adams, crashed in Alamo, California, taking his passenger down with him. The autopsy of the pilot showed a very recent myocardial infarction. O'Brien had been disqualified by the consultants previously because they believed he was too great a risk.

In the summer of 1986, Frank Rocks, an attorney representing American Airlines, having heard of Anders' resignation from the consultants' panel, called and asked him to testify in a coming trial. Frank Adams had released a senior American Airlines pilot to return to fly after having his aortic valve replaced. At that time the chance of stroke leading to sudden incapacitation with artificial aortic valves was extremely high. When the American Airlines medical department said, "No way, you cannot return to duty no matter what the FAA says," the pilot filed suit, and with the trial coming up they thought Anders would make a good witness.

The day of the trial in Dallas, with a courtroom full of reporters, Frank Rocks cleverly questioned Frank Adams' competence rather than that of American Airlines. When Anders testified as to his beliefs regarding Frank Adams' incompetence, the reporters of most major newspapers headlined his testimony, resulting in a detailed analysis of Adams' policies in the press and eventually a Congressional investigation. Finally, Adams' leadership of the FAA was terminated.

The new Federal Air Surgeon, John Jordan, asked Anders to return as a consultant a few months later, and Anders continued to serve for many years thereafter.

THIRTY-FOUR

THE BALLOON CATHETER AND THE HEART INSTITUTE

As Anders' research and reputation in exercise testing continued, he frequently was asked to present talks and meetings around the U.S. and Europe. In 1968, he met an intriguing fellow from Zurich, Switzerland, who had used a balloon on the tip of a catheter to open a narrowed coronary artery that he had created in a dog. Their meeting, at the American Heart Scientific Session in Miami, resulted in a friendship that would propel Anders into a new field. Dr. Andreas Grundzig explained that he needed help to develop this technique in humans and that he planned to spend time with Dick Mylar in San Francisco, who was also interested in this procedure. Within a few months Anders was visiting Dr. Mylar and observing the first use of this technique, called angioplasty, in humans. After a time Anders was trained by Mylar to use the balloon and by 1971 he brought the technique to Southern California.

The intervention attracted widespread attention as it promised to open up obstructed coronary arteries with a catheter, therefore reducing the need for a heart operation, which had, by that time, become a very commonly used modality. Cardiology, which had hardly been a specialty in the fifties, was now recognized as one of the most important in medicine, and the program at Long Beach

Memorial was recognized as one of the major centers in California and, indeed, in the nation.

Under the guidance of Grundzig and Mylar, angioplasty spread rapidly and became one of the most common cardiac procedures in the Western world. Anders' friendship with Mylar and Grundzig resulted in the rapid expansion of the technique at Memorial Hospital and provided another reason that the program assumed a leadership role in the community. But all was not a bed of roses.

Anders' success was resented by a number of the cardiologists who, in the early days, had been pleased to be recruited by Anders. They now complained to the administrators that Anders' role as director of the cardiac program gave him an unfair advantage. They decided that Anders, who by now had served as the chief of staff and whose medical group of twelve physicians had begun to have a good deal of influence, should not be allowed to compete against the others.

A committee was formed that eventually recommended that a new organizational structure be created, the Heart Institute. They recommended that the director would manage the organization and do cardiac research but would not be allowed to practice and, therefore, would not compete with the other cardiologists. This honor was offered to Anders. After considerable deliberation, Anders decided he might be able to promote the program he had initiated so many years ago more effectively from this new position, so he accepted.

His partners in the medical group he had so carefully nurtured for twenty-five years were furious. This was chiefly because Anders had consistently brought in the most income to the group, which was shared by everyone, and because his influence in the hospital had resulted in many in the group finding leadership roles. There would be many times that Anders would doubt the wisdom of his actions. With much fanfare the new Heart Institute was launched, and Anders recommended that his longtime patients go to his old partners for their care.

A new chest pain program was inaugurated to facilitate the better management of the many heart attack patients appearing in the emergency room, which required considerable organizational energy. For a time, Anders believed he had just possibly done the right thing. In 1986, however, his world began to unravel. A new hospital administrator, hired by the Board of Directors, vowed he would clean house. He would start with Anders, whose salary, Mr. Warren decided, was a waste of money. He offered Anders the option of retiring or being fired. The fact that Anders had built the heart program from scratch to one of international prominence was irrelevant to Mr. Warren. "Guys like you are a dime a dozen," he retorted. Anders was crushed. Although he was sixty-seven years old, he was not ready to retire. He was still going full-boar and would surely continue for years to come.

Anders was informed that he could stay on as Director of Research at a salary less than a hospital orderly if he went quietly without stirring up a fuss. Research had always been an important part of Anders' activity. By this time he had authored several books on stress testing and published 150 papers. He could continue this activity, which was very stimulating; however, if he went to war with Warren and lobbied the Board of Directors to keep his job as Heart Institute Director, he might lose the chance to continue something he loved to do. So he agreed to step down.

He moved out of the Director's office into an appropriately smaller one and resumed a limited private practice. His relationship with patients had always been an important part of his life and he was pleased with the opportunity to return to this. A couple of years went by, some of Anders' research activities and the return of many of his old patients took up a lot of his time, and life wasn't as dreary as he had feared. Then one day it was announced that Warren was leaving. Anders hoped he had been fired, but no one would say.

Shortly thereafter, the new administrator came to Anders with the offer of a new title, Careline Director. Although Anders was given little power, he assumed most of the work that had been left undone when the Medical Director's job was terminated. Finally, after several years, when it was decided that strong leadership was necessary in the Heart Institute, Anders was asked to take his old title back, Medical Director of the Heart Institute. He found that maybe his efforts on behalf of the program were appreciated more in his absence than while he was performing. Life is like that.

THIRTY-FIVE

THE TAKE-HOME MESSAGE

As Anders approached the end of his career in cardiology, he was asked to leave a message for the graduating class of the cardiology trainees at UC Irvine. Although he had learned over the years that young people rarely heeded the advice of their elders, he could not resist the opportunity to share some of his beliefs. Throughout his fifty years he had seen cardiology grow from a fledgling specialty to one of the most important in medicine. He had been part of a group of scientists who had participated in remarkable advances.

In the forties, very few types of heart disease had been treatable. Anders had seen dramatic changes in the diagnosis and treatment of coronary heart disease, valve disease, congenital heart disease, hypertension, abnormalities in rhythm, heart attacks, and heart failure. He had personally known many of those who had been responsible for these advances and had been recognized as a contributor to this progress. He was recognized for his textbooks, scientific papers, formal presentations, and leadership in cardiology societies.

What is the take-home message? A few items seem to have been paramount in his experience:

1) Never stop learning; it keeps you alert.

2) "It ain't necessarily so." The dogma of today is often tomorrow's discard.

3) A single observation, when viewed by an educated, open mind, can lead to a new understanding that can further the total body of knowledge. Remember Newton's observation of the falling apple; it led to our understanding of gravity.

4) Learn from history. Do not forget the dictum: "I can see farther by standing on the shoulders of giants."

5) Appreciate those who work hard at routine jobs. They make the world go around and facilitate the application of the achievements of those who are innovators.

6) A final note: You make a living by what you earn. You make a life by what you give.

— PHOTO GALLERY —

Anders at 5 years old

Max Dunovitz, Anders' childhood mentor

Yosemite Valley, where Anders worked in 1941

Anders in 1943 when he joined the Naval Reserve

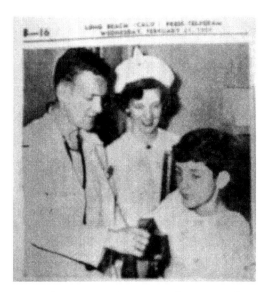

Anders in 1951 at Seaside Hospital

Anders at 50 years old

Anders and his wife at their farm, 1995

Memorial Hospital, 2000

WWW.CEDARVISTABOOKS.COM